NEVER

GIVE

UP

MICHAEL YOUSSEF

NEVER

GIVE

UP

 CHARISMA HOUSE

Scripture quotations from the World English Bible, public domain.

Visit the author's website at ltw.org, dryoussefbooks.com.

Cataloging-in-Publication Data is on file with the Library of Congress.
International Standard Book Number: 978-1-63641-088-3
E-book ISBN: 978-1-63641-089-0

22 23 24 25 26 — 9 8 7 6 5 4 3 2 1
Printed in the United States of America

To the great teachers at Moore Theological College—those who are still on earth and those who are already in heaven. To those godly men who between 1972 and 1975 not only taught me to love and revere the Word of God but also modeled for me what it is to never give up and tirelessly and persistently stand for biblical truth.

CONTENTS

FOREWORD

V ERY FEW TIMES over the course of a lifetime does a book come along that marks a defining moment in our lives. I look back over my own life to a handful of books that made indelible impressions on the formulation of my own convictions and helped set me on new and challenging adventures. I am confident and bold enough to say that *Never Give Up*, a new book by my longtime friend Dr. Michael Youssef, is just such a volume. This straightforward, no-holds-barred, hard-hitting book is a godsend to our evangelical community during these days of compromise and complacency.

Emerging from the old and often repeated words of the apostle Paul to his son in the ministry, Timothy, this book you now hold in your hands is the epitome of "power and a sound mind" wrapped in a package of love. While some speak the truth but not in love, and others speak in love avoiding the truth, Youssef loves us enough to speak the truth, and he does it in love.

If anyone anywhere at any time could write on this subject with authenticity and integrity, it is Dr. Michael Youssef. Born to a prominent evangelical family in Egypt, he resettled as a young man down under in Australia, resurfaced in America, and earned a terminal degree at one of the country's most prestigious institutions of higher learning, then founded and built one of the most far-reaching local churches in the Western world. Then he expanded the ministry he received from the Lord into a worldwide ministry. Indeed, his is a story against all odds, and he writes from the proven and credible platform of one who has never given up. So turn the page and read these words with the confidence that they flow from the pen of a man of impeccable integrity and influence whose own life is the essence of every word he has written in this volume.

These words are packed with an ingredient that is much needed in our day—truth! We never have to be afraid of the truth. It always wins in the end. So begin the journey. Read this book and reap its fruit—and *never give up*!

—O. S. HAWKINS
PRESIDENT AND CEO, GUIDESTONE

CHAPTER 1

ENCOURAGING WORDS FOR DISCOURAGING TIMES

GEORGE MÜLLER WAS a nineteenth-century Christian evangelist and the administrator of the Ashley Down orphanage in Bristol, England. He provided a home for more than ten thousand orphans over his lifetime and founded more than a hundred Christian schools. He was known as a man of prayer who always expected God to answer his prayers.

In November 1844 Müller made a commitment to pray for five friends, asking God to bring them to a saving faith in Jesus Christ. He prayed every day, whether he was at home or traveling, whether he was well or sick, no matter how busy his schedule. After a year and a half of daily prayer for these five friends, one of them gave his life to Christ. Müller thanked

God for answering his prayer, and he continued praying daily for the remaining four.

After five more years of praying, a second man came to Christ. Müller thanked God for the second answer to prayer and continued praying for the remaining three.

Six more years passed—and a third man came to Christ. By this time Müller had been praying more than a dozen years without missing a single day—and two of the five men he had prayed for remained unconverted. In 1880 he wrote in his diary, "But I hope in God, I pray on, and look for the answer. They are not converted yet, but they will be."

Müller died on March 10, 1898, at the age of ninety-two. He had been praying for the salvation of these men for fifty-four years. At the time of his death, the last two holdouts—two sons of one of Müller's friends—remained unsaved. Even so, Müller's prayers were answered, because they both committed their lives to Christ *after* his death.[1]

Müller patterned his prayer life after Jesus the Master, who taught His disciples to "always pray and not give up" (Luke 18:1). Müller never gave up—and neither should we.

Never give up on prayer.

Never give up on biblical truth.

Never give up on the infallibility of the Word of God.

Never give up on the faith that was once delivered.

Never give up on sound doctrine.

Press on, persevere, and don't ever give up.

One of the great examples of spiritual perseverance is the apostle Paul. Imprisoned in a cold Roman dungeon, Paul knew he was nearing the end of his life. Eager to leave a legacy, he wrote his final letter, addressing it to Timothy, a young church leader he had mentored in the faith. We know this letter today as 2 Timothy.

Paul was not writing to Timothy alone. He knew these inspired words would endure and be read by future generations. So this letter is truly an exhortation not only to Timothy, but to church leaders and church members today, including you and me.

The central theme of 2 Timothy is *never give up*. In every generation there are temptations to compromise God's truth. Falsehood and error creep into the church, tainting the purity of the Lord's gospel. The tendency to stray from God's truth was a major problem in the first-century church—and it has reached a crisis level in the twenty-first-century church.

AIM AT HEAVEN

McLean Bible Church was founded in an elementary school by five families in northern Virginia on Easter Sunday 1961. The founders declared the new church to be a Bible-believing evangelical congregation. It has grown into a multisite megachurch with locations all around the Washington, DC, metro area. From 1980 to 2017 the church was led by a theologically conservative preacher, Lon Solomon. In September 2017 Solomon stepped down to become pastor emeritus. His associate, David Platt, was promoted to lead pastor.

Soon after taking his new leadership position, Platt's teachings began to change. Platt and others in leadership at McLean Bible Church openly embraced secular-left social justice rhetoric. During the COVID-19 pandemic, when the church was under lockdown, several staffers joined a Washington, DC, Black Lives Matter (BLM) protest. Photos of staffers holding BLM signs were posted to the church's Facebook page, but the photos were later removed.[2]

While genuine Christians acknowledge that Black lives absolutely matter to Jesus and His church, the *organization* known as Black Lives Matter is totally incompatible with the Christian church. It is an anti-Christian, Marxist organization that has openly declared its commitment to disrupt "the Western prescribed nuclear family structure requirement."[3]

David Platt's "woke" social justice sermons seem to have provoked an exodus of Bible-believing members from the church, including many who had faithfully supported the church for decades. In May 2020 McLean Bible Church reported an average attendance of 12,154. One year later, average attendance had declined to 7,300 hundred, a drop of nearly 40 percent. The sudden drop in attendance led to steep budget cuts in missions, outreach, and church facilities.[4]

Both James White of Alpha and Omega Ministries (an evangelical apologetics organization) and conservative theologian Voddie Baucham, who is African American, describe Platt's teaching as an attempt to merge the Bible with critical race theory—a Marxist, race-conscious concept that attacks all institutions of society as inherently racist, rejects evidence and reason as "White" ways of knowing, and ranks people as either privileged or disadvantaged according to their race, gender, economic class, and so forth.[5]

When preachers decide that the pure, unadulterated gospel of Jesus Christ is not enough, they invite falsehood and error into the church. When preachers mix worldly political dogmas with the gospel, they lead the church down the road to hell.

The polluting of the gospel with secular politics is not only tragic, but it undermines the very social justice that "progressive Christians" wish to accomplish. If you want a morally righteous society, in which all people are treated with justice, compassion, and respect, then preach the uncompromised gospel of salvation through faith in Jesus Christ.

As C. S. Lewis noted, it was the early apostles who began the conversion of the Roman Empire, and it was the English evangelicals who abolished the slave trade. They didn't transform society by polluting the gospel with political and social theories. No, Lewis wrote—they "left their mark on Earth, precisely because their minds were occupied with Heaven. It is since Christians have largely ceased to think of the other world that they have become so ineffective in this. Aim at Heaven and you will get earth 'thrown in': aim at earth and you will get neither."[6]

As Jesus said, "If you hold to my teaching, you are really my disciples" (John 8:31).

NO ROOM FOR DISAGREEMENT

In December 2019 the Church of England appointed Stephen Cottrell as archbishop of York, the second-highest position in the Anglican church. Many in the so-called "progressive" wing of the church celebrated this appointment because Cottrell has been an outspoken supporter of gay rights within the church. But those who are committed to remaining faithful to biblical truth took a different view. For example, Andrea Williams, an Anglican and the chief executive of Christian Concern, the United Kingdom's most prominent evangelical organization, responded, "This is not a bishop who respects biblical truth when it comes to human sexuality or marriage."[7]

Of course, every person deserves to be treated with respect and kindness. We are all sinners, and God loves the homosexual sinner as much as He loves the heterosexual sinner. So as Christians we are to love everyone with the same unconditional love that Christ has shown to us. But we don't do sinners any favors by normalizing or celebrating sin, or by denying the teaching of Scripture.

The Scriptures make clear, in such passages

as Leviticus 18:22 and 20:13, Romans 1:26–27, 1 Corinthians 6:9–11, and 1 Timothy 1:8–11, that homosexual behavior is a sin. We must treat homosexual people with Christlike love and respect, just as Jesus treated the woman caught in adultery with love and respect. But we remember that He also told her, "Go now and leave your life of sin" (John 8:11).

That is not how Stephen Cottrell, the archbishop of York, treats the issue of homosexuality. He takes the position that human wisdom supersedes the wisdom of God. He supports what Anglican progressives call a "radical new Christian inclusion." He claims that the church damages itself by rejecting the secular view of human sexuality. The world now views the church as "immoral," he says, because of biblical teaching on homosexuality. The biblical view of same-sex relationships, he says, is "homophobic"—a buzzword intended to prejudice the argument and frame Bible-believing Christians as "phobic" (afraid of homosexual people).

Archbishop Cottrell claims Bible passages that condemn homosexual behavior are merely "part of our story and our inheritance." He says that "what we know now about human development and human sexuality requires us to look again at those texts to see what they are actually saying to our situation, for what we know now is not what was known then."[8] In other words, we in the twenty-first century know so much more about human sexuality than God did when He inspired the writing of His Word.

Or maybe it would be more accurate to say

Archbishop Cottrell believes God's Word is not inspired at all but is merely a collection of ancient stories and opinions we can safely ignore. Either way, the archbishop of York has explicitly departed from the traditional teachings of the church and a common-sense understanding of the Scriptures.

Worst of all, he has made it clear that there is no room for disagreement with his position on homosexuality. Anglican clergy have said that on more than one occasion Archbishop Cottrell stood before a meeting of clergy and declared that anyone who disagreed with the progressive view of human sexuality should leave the church. Clergy who hold the biblical view of human sexuality are not welcome in today's Church of England.[9]

We have come a long way since the time of the English reformers, who willingly went to the stake to be burned to death rather than betray the Holy Scriptures.

BLOOM WHERE YOU ARE PLANTED

Today, as in past generations, churches and individual Christians are tempted to compromise God's truth and pollute the gospel of Jesus Christ with worldly ideas. That's why the central theme of 2 Timothy— *never give up* on the truth of God's Word—is so vitally important today.

If I were to assess the evangelical church in the

Western world, I would compare it to a botanical hothouse. A hothouse is a structure with glass walls and a glass roof with heating equipment so that a specific temperature can be maintained. This way, even in wintertime, warm-weather plants can be grown at a constant temperature. The gardener will come in and test the soil, add just the right amount of fertilizer and water, and may even play classical music on the stereo to keep the plants in a cheerful mood.

But the moment you take a hothouse plant out into the real world, where it is too hot or too cold, or the soil is too arid or there's too much rain, the plant will sicken and die before your eyes. That is how I see the professing church in the twenty-first century.

The Bible tells us that when we are rooted and established in the Word of God, we will bloom wherever we are planted. (See Colossians 2:6–7.) If you are planted in Pharaoh's prison, you will rise up to become the prime minister of Egypt. (See Genesis 39:7–20; 41:37–44.) If you are planted in the fiery furnace, you will rise up and testify before the king. (See Daniel 3:9–30.) If you are planted in a den of lions, you will rise up to become second-in-command of the Persian empire. (See Daniel 6.) If you are planted in the desert, you will bloom and proclaim that God is with us. (See Matthew 3:1–2.)

When Paul began writing his final letter, he was planted in a wretched Roman prison. Yet the pages of his letter bloom with a rich and encouraging meaning for our lives today. Paul wrote:

Paul, an apostle of Christ Jesus by the will of God, in keeping with the promise of life that is in Christ Jesus,

To Timothy, my dear son:

Grace, mercy and peace from God the Father and Christ Jesus our Lord.

I thank God, whom I serve, as my ancestors did, with a clear conscience, as night and day I constantly remember you in my prayers. Recalling your tears, I long to see you, so that I may be filled with joy. I am reminded of your sincere faith, which first lived in your grandmother Lois and in your mother Eunice and, I am persuaded, now lives in you also.

For this reason I remind you to fan into flame the gift of God, which is in you through the laying on of my hands. For the Spirit God gave us does not make us timid, but gives us power, love and self-discipline.

—2 TIMOTHY 1:1–7

These words become especially meaningful to us when we realize where Paul was and what his circumstances were when he wrote them.

STAND UP AND FIGHT

From the Book of Acts and other historical accounts, we know Paul was imprisoned twice in Rome. His first imprisonment was a house arrest in a rented place where Paul was allowed to receive visitors. He was eventually freed, probably for lack of evidence. After his first imprisonment, Paul likely went into Spain to preach the gospel.

Paul was arrested and imprisoned a second time during the great persecution of Nero, the fifth emperor of Rome. Nero blamed the Christians for the Great Fire of Rome July AD 64. Paul's second imprisonment was not like the first. Denied the privilege of house arrest, the apostle was sent to Mamertine Prison, a dark and miserable dungeon carved out of the northeastern slope of the Capitoline Hill. His sufferings were magnified by age and physical infirmity.

My wife and I have visited Mamertine Prison several times. We have stood on the very stone floor where Paul languished in his final days. There is a hole in the center of the ceiling through which food and water were lowered to Paul. There are no windows. The place is cold and damp, close and claustrophobic. My wife and I couldn't stay there for long.

What would be the furthest thing from a snug and cozy hothouse environment? It would have to be the apostle Paul's cell at Mamertine Prison.

We don't know how long the apostle Paul remained in that miserable place. But we know he was eventually taken to the place of execution on the Ostian Way. There he knelt with his gray head resting upon a great stone. Moments later, the executioner swung his axe down upon the apostle's neck—and Paul passed from this life into the presence of the Lord.

Some weeks or months before the Roman government took his earthly life, Paul wrote these moving words to his spiritual son, Timothy—and to generations of believers yet unborn. I'm grateful to the Lord for preserving these treasured words. Because of 2 Timothy, we can know triumph in times of defeat, we can know joy in the pit of despair, and we can find encouragement in times of disappointment.

Paul knew his disciple Timothy very well. He knew Timothy's strengths and weaknesses. He knew Timothy was prone to discouragement, self-pity, and the temptation to surrender. Timothy also tended to be timid and unassertive in situations that called for boldness. He sometimes allowed unscrupulous people to take advantage of him.

So Paul wrote to Timothy from the depths of the dungeon and urged his young friend to *never give up the fight*. As Paul contemplated his departure from this life, his message was: stand up and fight for the truth, regardless of the cost.

In each of the four chapters of 2 Timothy, Paul unveiled a unique aspect of what it means to never give up on biblical truth. In chapter 1, Paul urges us to uphold God's truth at all costs. In chapter 2, he enjoins us to be unafraid of suffering for God's truth. In chapter 3, he encourages us to be steadfast even when others fall away from God's truth. In chapter 4, he tells us to maintain our sense of urgency in spreading the good news to others.

I'm convinced there is no more urgent message for Christians in the twenty-first century than Paul's second and final letter to Timothy.

These days we see so many people, including leaders in the church, turning their backs on God's truth. If I focused only on the apostasy I see all around me, I could sink into a deep spiritual depression.

But I am not depressed. I am joyful and encouraged! Why? Because I look around me and I see God raising up a new generation of young Timothys. I see bold young men and women in the church who are unashamed of the truth of the gospel. I'm convinced they will guard God's truth and remain faithful until Jesus returns.

PREPARED TO BELIEVE

Paul opens his letter with the words, "Paul, an apostle of Christ Jesus by the will of God, in keeping with the promise of life that is in Christ Jesus."

Apostles were people who had a unique calling of Jesus Christ upon their lives. The twelve apostles of the New Testament derived their apostolic authority from the experience of seeing the risen Lord. In the Bible, only a person who had met Jesus face to face was qualified to be an apostle.

Unlike the other apostles, Paul never met Jesus prior to the crucifixion and resurrection. Instead, Paul's face-to-face encounter with Jesus took place years after the resurrection. Paul was a fanatical persecutor of the early Christians. Just two or three years after the resurrection, when Paul was on the road to Damascus in Syria, he experienced a dramatic encounter with the resurrected Lord (Acts 9). On the Damascus road, Jesus not only revealed Himself to Paul, but He commissioned Paul. That's why Paul was not afraid to die for Jesus. He knew that it is a joyful experience to die *in* Jesus.

Paul addressed this letter, "To Timothy, my dear son" (v. 2). Timothy was not Paul's biological son, but his spiritual son. Timothy came to the Lord through the ministry of the apostle Paul, so Paul became Timothy's spiritual father.

I can identify with Paul, because my goal is to someday arrive in heaven with more than a million sons and daughters in Christ—a million people from around the world whom God has allowed me to introduce to Jesus.

Paul goes on to write some of the most intensely personal words in any of his letters: "I constantly remember you in my prayers" (v. 3). Not occasionally. Not merely when you happen to come to mind. No, Paul prays for Timothy *constantly*, again and again throughout the day.

And Paul says he recalls Timothy's tears (v. 4). Those tears speak of Timothy's sincere and tender heart, his genuine faith, and his godly affection for Paul and other believers. That tenderhearted faith came from Timothy's godly heritage. He had a godly mother and grandmother who taught him from the Scriptures and prepared him to receive the message of the gospel.

If you are a mother, father, or grandparent, please take Paul's words to heart. It is profoundly important that we sow seeds of faith in the hearts of our children and grandchildren. If we sow those seeds now while they are young and their hearts are receptive, they will bear fruit someday. You may not see the fruit immediately—much as George Müller didn't see the results of his prayers for many years—but keep praying, keep sharing your faith, keep teaching them the Word of God, and sooner or later you will see the fruit of God's Spirit in their lives.

Timothy's grandmother Lois and his mother, Eunice, undoubtedly taught him the Old Testament passages about the coming of the Messiah. So when Paul taught Timothy that the Messiah had already come and fulfilled the Old Testament prophecies, Timothy's heart was prepared. He could look at the Old Testament prophecies and compare them side by side with the gospel of Jesus Christ, and he could see that the prophecies had been fulfilled.

The Messiah had come.

His name is Jesus.

He died on the cross and rose again.

He ascended into heaven.

And He will come back to judge the human race.

Because his heart had been so well prepared by his mother and grandmother, Timothy readily placed his faith in Jesus.

POWERFUL
ENCOURAGEMENT

We know Timothy's father was a Gentile (that is, a non-Jew, possibly a Greek). So Timothy's father was not a Jewish believer like his mother. But here's an encouraging word I want you to notice. Timothy's mother is a living example of a principle Paul taught in 1 Corinthians 7:14: in a family with a believing spouse and a nonbelieving spouse, the believer *sanctifies* both the nonbelieving spouse and the children.

This doesn't mean the nonbeliever and children are *saved* by the believing spouse. *Sanctify* means "to set apart to a sacred purpose."[10] Every human being, in order to be saved, must make a personal decision to accept Jesus as Lord. But the faith of a believing parent does sanctify and set apart the children as holy and consecrated to the Lord.

And there's more. Paul vividly remembers the day he and other elders prayed for Timothy by the laying on of hands (v. 6). At that time Timothy received the Holy Spirit, was gifted by the Holy Spirit, and went on to exercise his gifts through the Holy Spirit. So Paul, the great encourager, tells Timothy, in effect, "I remember all of that, Timothy, and I thank God for you." Timothy, who was prone to discouragement, must have been greatly encouraged and strengthened by those words. Paul's encouragement empowered young Timothy to stand firm against the onslaught of Satan.

Friend in Christ, the same Satan who opposed Timothy and provoked feelings of discouragement in him is still active in the world today. Right now Satan may be tempting you to throw in the towel, to give up, to surrender. And candidly, there is a lot in this world to be discouraged about. We face health fears, career worries, problems raising our kids, plus mounting bills and debts. All around us we see political squabbling, racial strife, soaring national debt, rising crime, threats of wars and terrorism, inflation and unemployment, and global instability.

It would be so easy to give in to discouragement and say, "Lord, don't ask me to be a witness for You. Don't ask me to share You with my neighbors and coworkers. I'm just going to lock my door, mind my own business, and let the world go by."

That's Satan talking. It's Satan who wants to instill in us a spirit of fear, timidity, and discouragement. Don't listen to the voice of Satan, the voice of discouragement.

Instead, listen to the Spirit of God. Take out your Bible and read words of encouragement. Remember how God blessed you before. Remember how He protected you and watched over you and rescued you.

Can you remember a time when you fell into a pit of circumstances from which there seemed no escape? How did God rescue you? Meditate on that experience, thank God for His protection in your life, and tell Him you look forward to seeing how He will redeem you from your present situation.

The same God who rescued Joseph from an Egyptian prison, the same God who rescued Daniel from the lion's den, the same God who rescued you from your circumstances in the past, this same God wants to bless you, encourage you, and use you again.

THE HEART OF
PAUL'S MESSAGE

This brings us to the very heart of Paul's encouragement to Timothy in the opening verses of this letter. He tells Timothy, in effect, "Shake off your timidity, shake off your fear, shake off your discouragement!" Why? Paul explains in verse 7: "For the Spirit God gave us *does not make us timid*, but gives us power, love and self-discipline" (emphasis added). In some translations, "self-discipline" is translated "a sound mind."

I could write an entire book on this verse alone—and someday, perhaps, I will. But for now, I'll do my best to summarize Paul's profound insight.

Paul is saying, first, God will *never* send an evil spirit to make us afraid. I don't know how many demons there are in the spiritual realm carrying out the bidding of Satan. And it doesn't matter. What does matter is that we recognize that feelings of fear, anxiety, and timidity are not from the Spirit of God. Such feelings may arise from our unstable human emotions or from Satan and his demons.

The Bible tells us, "You, dear children, are from God and have overcome them, because *the one who is in you* is greater than the one who is in the world" (1 John 4:4, emphasis added). Who is "the one who is in you"? The Holy Spirit. Who is "the one who is in the world"? Satan. Satan wants to crush your effectiveness, neutralize your impact, paralyze your spiritual life, and terrify you, trapping you in a prison of fear.

But the Spirit of God within you is greater than the spirit of fear. The Holy Spirit dwells within you to encourage and empower you to say "No!" to fear, to say "Go away!" to Satan.

We can't help but notice the irony of Paul's message of encouragement to Timothy. There is Paul, awaiting death in the most miserable dungeon in Rome—and his message to Timothy and us is, *Don't lock yourself up in a prison of fear.*

Paul is saying, in effect, "If you live in fear, your prison is much worse than mine. If you live in fear, you live in a cage colder and more unbreakable than steel. If you live in fear, you are trapped in a prison more escape-proof than Alcatraz or Devil's Island."

If you let fear rule your life, it will waste your God-given abilities, inhibit your desire to serve God, paralyze your commitment to God, and impede your spiritual growth. Fear can damage and ruin your friendships, family relationships, and marriage relationship. Fear can undermine your health, disturb your sleep, raise your blood pressure, ruin your digestion, and shorten your life.

That's why Paul tells Timothy—and us—that God's Spirit is the Spirit of comfort, encouragement, and boldness. The devil is a liar. God's Spirit is the Spirit of truth.

We often don't like to admit that we are afraid, so we may excuse our fear and call it by different names. We might say, "I'm careful," "I'm cautious," "I'm shy," "I lack confidence," "God didn't give me an outgoing personality," "I'm just not an adventuresome person," "I can't share the gospel with my neighbors because God didn't give me the gift of evangelism," or "Other people are so much better at serving others; I would just make a mess of things."

We can try to give our fearfulness another name, but we can't escape the truth. We don't have to live in fear. Paul has shown us the way to conquer our fear and timidity.

THE ANTIDOTE TO FEAR

Please understand, there is nothing sinful about experiencing fear when you face real danger. If you see a truck rushing at you while you're in a crosswalk, a surge of fear and adrenaline will put power in your muscles as you leap out of harm's way. That instantaneous impulse of self-preservation we call fear is intended to keep us safe.

Believe me, I know that impulse well. I have experienced raw fear in dangerous situations, and that's a normal emotion in the face of an immediate threat. But in those moments, I have also experienced the Spirit of God breathing within me, saying, "Fear not!"

Again and again throughout the Gospels, in various ways and at various times, Jesus tells His followers, "Fear not!"

- "You of little faith, why are you so afraid?" (Matt. 8:26).

- "So do not be afraid of them" (Matt. 10:26).

- "Take courage! It is I. Don't be afraid" (Matt. 14:27).

- "Why are you so afraid? Do you still have no faith?" (Mark 4:40).

- "Don't be afraid; just believe" (Mark 5:36).

- "Don't be afraid; from now on you will fish for people" (Luke 5:10).

- "Don't be afraid; just believe, and she will be healed" (Luke 8:50).

- "Do not be afraid, little flock, for your Father has been pleased to give you the kingdom" (Luke 12:32).

- "Peace I leave with you; my peace I give you. I do not give to you as the world gives. Do not let your hearts be troubled and do not be afraid" (John 14:27).

We don't have to be afraid of life. Why? Because Jesus said, "I am the way and the truth and the life"

(John 14:6). He is the author of life, and every detail and aspect of our lives is under His control.

We don't have to be afraid of death. Why? Because Jesus said, "I am the Living One; I was dead, and now look, I am alive for ever and ever! And I hold the keys of death and Hades" (Rev. 1:18).

We don't have to fear the unknown. Why? Because Jesus said, "I am the Alpha and the Omega, the First and the Last, the Beginning and the End" (Rev. 22:13). He is the Creator of time and space, the future and the past, and there is nothing in life unknown to Him.

If there is one thing the apostle Paul learned in more than three decades of walking with the Lord, serving the Lord, and preaching the gospel of Jesus Christ, it is this—there is only one antidote to fear: faith in the almighty God who alone can banish fear from our lives.

God is in control. He never makes a mistake. And His love never fails.

LIVING CONFIDENTLY
AND FEARLESSLY

Do you feel you are living effectively for Jesus? Are you serving joyfully? Are you witnessing eagerly? Are you giving generously? If not, why? What is hindering your effectiveness for the Lord?

Is it fear? Are you afraid of failure? Are you afraid of being ridiculed or mocked for your faith? Do you lack confidence in sharing your faith?

Believe me, it is better to obey God, take a step of risky faith, and fall flat on your face than never risk at all. If fear of failure keeps you from attempting great things for God, consider this: if you never take the risk, you're defeated before you begin.

Everybody fails from time to time—at least everybody who makes an attempt. Falling down doesn't make you a failure. *Staying* down does.

Failure is never your undertaker. It is only your teacher.

Failure is never a dead-end street for believers. It is only a detour.

People have said to me, "I can't serve Christ. My past sins haunt me." If your sins are covered by the blood of Jesus, God has buried them in the depths of the deepest sea. What's more, He has placed a sign over that spot that reads, "No fishing allowed!"

A verse to memorize for times when Satan brings up past sins to intimidate and immobilize you is Isaiah 54:17, which says, "'No weapon forged against you will prevail, and you will refute every tongue that accuses you. This is the heritage of the servants of the LORD, and this is their vindication from me,' declares the LORD." For times when you face threats, obstacles, and enemies, remember Psalm 27:1. It says, "The LORD is my light and my salvation—whom shall I fear? The LORD is the stronghold of my life—of whom shall I be afraid?"

When I was in my early teens, there was a street bully who used to intimidate me. My parents raised me to avoid fighting because Christians should be peacemakers, not fighters. So this street bully knew he could push me around and I wouldn't fight back. He continued to bully me week after week.

One day I was walking down the street with my oldest brother, Nader, and I saw the bully standing on the street corner. Nader was six feet five inches and, like me, had been taught at home that Christians shouldn't fight. But the bully didn't know that.

So, with my brother close behind me, I walked up to the bully and stared him down.

The bully looked at me.

Then he looked at Nader.

Then he turned and ran like a jackrabbit.

My friend, fear is a street bully. Fear will intimidate you if you let it. But we don't have to let fear rule over us.

We have a spiritual big brother. His name is Jesus. And every satanic, demonic bully flees at the name of Jesus. Call on Jesus whenever you are afraid, and then watch your fears flee in panic.

Though Satan is a street bully in this world, his power over us is limited by the limitless power of God. And we know the Spirit God has given us does not make us timid, but gives us power, love, self-discipline, and a sound mind.

So live confidently and fearlessly in the power of the Holy Spirit.

CHAPTER 2

DO NOT BE ASHAMED

O<small>N</small> M<small>AY</small> 25, 2021, Leesburg (Virginia) Elementary School teacher Byron "Tanner" Cross stood before the Loudoun County School Board and said, "I love all of my students, but I will never lie to them, regardless of the consequences. I'm a teacher, but I serve God first, and I will not affirm that a biological boy can be a girl and vice versa because it's against my religion, it's lying to my child, it's abuse to a child, and it's sinning against our God."

Cross also referred to a *60 Minutes* episode in which young people who had identified as transgender and undergone life-altering surgery and/or hormone treatment later regretted their decision and wanted to return to their original gender. Many in the counseling and medical community are motivated by profit or political fanaticism to push confused young people to make self-destructive choices. Cross told the school board he was "speaking out of love for those who suffer with gender dysphoria" (gender-based depression and confusion).

Two days after speaking to the school board, Cross was suspended from his job as an elementary school physical education specialist. He was being disciplined for opposing the school system's Policy 8040, which stated school staff and students were required to use the "chosen name and gender pronouns" that "gender-expansive or transgender students" preferred.[1]

In case you haven't kept up with the bewildering array of gender pronouns currently in use, gender-expansive or transgender people may demand that you call a biological male "her," a biological female "him," or possibly "they," "themself," "sie," "hir," "hirself," "zie," "zir," or "zirself."[2] My point is not to ridicule people with gender-identity issues. Far from it. My heart goes out to people who struggle with their gender identity, and we must love all people with the love of Christ, including those who label themselves LGBTQ+.

Friend in Christ, the emotional and spiritual health of your children and grandchildren is under assault as never before in human history. As early as preschool and kindergarten, children are being exposed to radical, destructive sexual ideas as a part of taxpayer-funded public school curriculum.

In fact, your children may have already been exposed to the Gender Unicorn, an innocent-seeming purple cartoon creature with hearts on its chest, a DNA helix for its private parts, and rainbows all around. It was first adopted by the Charlotte, North Carolina, school district and has spread across America and into Canada. The purple unicorn leads children through a process of choosing their own "gender identity" and choosing the gender they are "attracted to." One official for the Oregon Department of Education gushed over the program, saying, "We have more and more kindergartners coming out and identifying."[3]

Are you kidding me? Kindergartners! Five-year-old children are "coming out" and "identifying" as some other gender besides their biological sex? How would kindergartners (who are prepubescent and never have thoughts of sex unless the subject is forced on them by evil-minded grown-ups) identify their sexuality? The only way that could happen is if ideologically twisted "educators" *impose* such ideas on children.

And that is exactly what is taking place through such perverted propaganda as the Gender Unicorn. This is nothing less than child abuse perpetrated by government education on an entire generation of children, including your children and grandchildren.

SATANIC DOCTRINES

Genesis 5:2 tells us that God "created them male and female and blessed them." In 1 Corinthians 5:1, Paul warns the church against sexual immorality, which brings shame upon the church.

In Romans 1, Paul states that God's wrath "is being revealed from heaven against all the godlessness and wickedness of people, who suppress the truth by their wickedness" (v. 18). People are without excuse, Paul adds, because "although they knew God, they neither glorified him as God nor gave thanks to him, but their thinking became futile and their foolish hearts were darkened. Although they claimed to be wise, they became fools....Because of this, God gave them over to shameful lusts" (vv. 21–22, 26).

The people Paul describes in Romans 1 are the very people who are imposing these vile ideas on children in the public schools. My heart aches for schoolchildren today. Children from non-Christian homes are vulnerable to indoctrination by godless "educators." There is nothing to shield them from the satanic doctrines that dominate government education today. That's why so many young people are accepting the notion that they are not male or female, but gay, bi, trans, two-spirited, intersexual, pansexual, gender-fluid, and on and on.

Meanwhile, teachers and students from Christian homes are under enormous pressure to set aside their beliefs, yield to social pressure, and cooperate with the godless educational system. Teachers and students who stand for biblical truth are under attack. They are shamed for proclaiming biblical truth. They are persecuted for living out godly principles.

As Christians, we must stand with parents, teachers, and children. We need more brave teachers who will risk their careers and reputations to defend biblical truth. We need Christian teachers who will band together and defy godless school boards and say, "We stand for biblical truth. We stand for the emotional and sexual health of our students. We won't let you pick us off one by one. We stand together and you'll have to fire us all."

Take a bold stand for righteousness and God's truth. That's the theme of the next section of 2 Timothy.

SHAME—THE "MASTER EMOTION"

Paul continues his message of encouragement to Timothy—a message that still speaks to young and old alike in the twenty-first century:

> So do not be ashamed of the testimony about our Lord or of me his prisoner. Rather, join with me in suffering for the gospel, by the power of God. He has saved us and called us to a holy life—not because of anything we have done but because of his own purpose and grace. This grace was given us in Christ Jesus before the beginning of time, but it has now been revealed through the appearing of our Savior, Christ Jesus, who has destroyed death and has brought life and immortality to light through the gospel. And of this gospel I was appointed a herald and an apostle and a teacher. That is why I am suffering as I am. Yet this is no cause for shame, because I know whom I have believed, and am convinced that he is able to guard what I have entrusted to him until that day.
>
> What you heard from me, keep as the pattern of sound teaching, with faith and love in

Christ Jesus. Guard the good deposit that was entrusted to you—guard it with the help of the Holy Spirit who lives in us.

You know that everyone in the province of Asia has deserted me, including Phygelus and Hermogenes.

May the Lord show mercy to the household of Onesiphorus, because he often refreshed me and was not ashamed of my chains. On the contrary, when he was in Rome, he searched hard for me until he found me. May the Lord grant that he will find mercy from the Lord on that day! You know very well in how many ways he helped me in Ephesus.

—2 TIMOTHY 1:8–18

Paul tells Timothy, "Do not be ashamed of the testimony about our Lord or of me his prisoner" (v. 8). The word *shame* has been turned upside down in our time. Things we used to be ashamed of we now speak of with pride. And things we used to take pride in are now considered shameful.

Our culture has rejected biblical definitions of shame, replacing them with worldly definitions. This change began in the 1990s. In the February 1992 edition of *The Atlantic*, psychologist/psychoanalyst Robert Karen observed, "Thirty, fifty, a hundred years ago, shame was a part of our common conversation. The literature of the nineteenth century, from Austen to Tolstoy, was full of it. Parents warned their children about anything that might incur it—adultery or illegitimate pregnancy, cowardice or failure, bad manners, laziness, dirty underwear. When shame struck, it was typically a feeling akin to being caught out in the open and desperately wanting to hide."

By the 1990s, Dr. Karen noted, the subject of shame was everywhere in psychological literature and was seen as "the master emotion," the invisible regulator of our emotions. He explained: "Current research identifies shame as an important element in aggression (including the violence of wife-beaters), in addictions, obsessions, narcissism, depression, and numerous other psychiatric syndromes....Many psychologists now believe that shame is the preeminent cause of emotional distress in our time."[4]

How did the psychology and psychoanalysis community respond to this new view of shame as "the master emotion"? They claimed that if we could just remove shame from people, we could cure violence, addiction, and other psychiatric and social ills. So the psychological community focused on eradicating shame. Accordingly, many people no longer feel shame while committing shameful acts. Instead, they take pride in what the Bible condemns as shameful.

BELIEVING A LIE
ABOUT OURSELVES

How does the Bible define shame? Biblically, shame is a healthy response to sin. When we sin, a healthy conscience listens to the conviction of the Holy Spirit, and the Spirit provokes a healthy sense of shame in us. That feeling of shame drives us to repentance—a sincere change of heart that leads us away from sin and back toward God.

There is healthy shame and unhealthy shame. Healthy shame comes from the realization that we have violated our conscience and sinned against God. Healthy shame can be instantly cleansed through a prayer of confession and sincere repentance.

Unhealthy shame is a result of a person's inability to accept the grace and forgiveness of God. A person experiencing unhealthy shame doesn't merely say, "I failed," but says, "I am a failure, and I don't deserve forgiveness."

Ultimately, unhealthy shame is the result of believing a lie about ourselves. People with unhealthy shame reject themselves and respond with self-hate and self-reproach. Unhealthy shame leads to self-destruction. It drives us to alcoholism, food addiction, drug addiction, pornography addiction, and other addictive behaviors we use to silence the voice of shame within us.

A person with healthy shame rejects sin and responds with repentance. Healthy shame leads to repentance, forgiveness, joy, and fulfillment. Healthy shame brings life and healing.

But it's unhealthy to be ashamed of the gospel. As Paul would tell you, "Please do *not* be ashamed of biblical truth. Please do *not* be ashamed of biblical morality. Please do *not* be ashamed when the godless people of this world persecute you and call you names. Please do *not* let this fallen world shame you for believing in what is good, godly, and true."

As we look at this passage, it's important to understand that shame, fear, and timidity are cousins. They are part of the same family. We saw in chapter 1 of this book that Paul is writing his last legacy from a lowly Roman dungeon. He is telling Timothy and us to never give up on biblical truth, never be afraid to stand up for God's truth, and never forsake the gospel to win favor with other people.

Paul tells Timothy in verse 8, "So do not be ashamed of the testimony about our Lord or of me his prisoner. Rather, join with me in suffering for the gospel, by the power of God."

EMBARRASSED "CHRISTIANS"

There are many self-described "Christians" today who are ashamed of God's truth, so they have substituted human wisdom for God's truth. They are embarrassed by the Lord's teachings about judgment and hell, so they have invented a lot of new teachings that have eliminated judgment and eternal punishment. They think they have invented a new form of Christianity that will be more palatable to worldly thinking. But all they have done is pollute the gospel, leaving nothing worth believing in.

Some are embarrassed by the miracles in the Bible. They are ashamed of the claim that Jesus was crucified for our sins and rose from the dead. They say, "This is the twenty-first century! No one believes in miracles anymore. Let's just focus on the good things Jesus said and try to live by His teachings."

The problem is that Jesus taught primarily about Himself, about sacrificing Himself for our sins, about His death and resurrection, and about coming again to judge the human race. If you are ashamed of the miracles of Jesus, then you must be ashamed of the gospel of Jesus—and you are left with nothing to believe in.

As we will see later in his letter to Timothy, Paul speaks of people who have "a form of godliness but denying its power." He adds, "Have nothing to do with such people" (2 Tim. 3:5). These are people who say to the world, "Are you ashamed of the teachings of Jesus and Paul? Are you ashamed of the miracles in the Bible? Well, so am I! Let's just cut all those embarrassing parts out of the Bible and only focus on the parts of the Bible that are relevant today, the parts that are consistent with a secular, political, and social agenda. It won't *really* be Christianity, but we can still *call* it Christianity and pretend it's the real thing."

These false Christians use many different labels for themselves and their false teachings: progressive Christians, postmodern Christians, emerging church, generous orthodoxy, red-letter Christians, post-evangelical Christians, and on and on. They think that by watering down Christianity to make it more palatable to worldly thinking, they are doing the gospel a favor. But the apostle Paul begs to differ.

Paul appeals directly to Timothy, you, and me

when he writes, "Do not be ashamed of the testimony about our Lord." He is telling us, in effect, "*Do not* sell out! *Do not* compromise biblical truth! *Do not* be embarrassed by the gospel of Jesus Christ. *Do not* be ashamed of the Word of God. *Do not* repackage the gospel to make it more acceptable to ungodly people. *Do not* back away from the gospel truth regardless of all the persecution, ridicule, and hostility this world throws at you."

The Bible does not waste words. If Timothy had not been tempted to compromise the gospel, Paul would not have given him this word of exhortation. I believe Paul even had to deal with the temptation to compromise in his own heart. That's why he felt it necessary to boldly proclaim in Romans 1:16, "For *I am not ashamed of the gospel*, because it is the power of God that brings salvation to everyone who believes: first to the Jew, then to the Gentile" (emphasis added). I believe Paul made such a strong point of not being ashamed of the gospel precisely because he wrestled with this temptation, faced it, and conquered it.

Jesus fully understood that His followers would be tempted by feelings of embarrassment and shame regarding the gospel of salvation. That's why He warned us in Mark 8:38, "If anyone is ashamed of me and my words in this adulterous and sinful generation, the Son of Man will be ashamed of them when he comes in his Father's glory with the holy angels."

It's normal to be concerned about what other people think of us. I experience it. So do you. We may not want to admit it, but it's easier to go with the flow than to swim against the current. It's easier to go along to get along. When people around us express ungodly opinions or make dirty jokes, it's easier to nod and laugh in agreement than to take a bold moral stand. It's easier to wink at sin than to confront it. It's easier to let our kids get away with sin than to lovingly discipline them.

Most of all, it's easier to remain quiet and allow the world to go to hell than to speak up, witness to our neighbors, and save them from a Christless eternity.

Self-affirmation is easier than self-examination. It's easier to post recipes and pictures of puppies on social media than to post messages of the good news of salvation.

The Christian gospel calls us to transcend our fear and embarrassment and to boldly confess before men and women that Jesus Christ is Lord. It may mean we will be ridiculed. It may mean we will be persecuted. It may mean we will lose our jobs. But what did the gospel cost our Lord?

LIFE AND IMMORTALITY
THROUGH THE GOSPEL

In the Garden of Gethsemane, Jesus asked the Father, "Abba, Father…everything is possible for you. Take this cup from me. Yet not what I will, but what you will" (Mark 14:36). He prayed three times for some way to escape the cross. Each time, the Father's answer was silence—which was the same as no. (This is an important lesson to remember when our own prayers are met with silence. If God said no to the prayers of His Son, we should not feel it's unfair when God says no to our petitions.)

Jesus was obedient and willing to bear the shame of a criminal's death, the shame of bearing all the sins of the human race. Jesus was willing to undergo a depth of humiliation, suffering, and shame that you and I cannot begin to understand.

But Peter, the most bold and outspoken of the twelve disciples of Jesus, was unwilling to taste of the cup that Jesus drank. While Jesus was on trial, Peter warmed himself by the fire in the courtyard of Caiaphas' house. A servant girl confronted Peter and said, "You also were with that Nazarene, Jesus." Peter was ashamed to be identified with Christ. "'I don't know or understand what you're talking about,' he said" (Mark 14:67–68).

The servant girl wouldn't let up. She continued to accuse him of being a follower of Jesus. Three times Peter denied knowing Him.

On the night before the crucifixion, Peter was ashamed to acknowledge he was a follower of Jesus Christ. After the resurrection, Peter would become the boldest and bravest of all the apostles. Tradition tells us that Peter died on a cross, crucified upside down because he declared himself unworthy to die in the same manner as the Lord.

No matter what the world does to us, we must

never be ashamed of the gospel of Jesus Christ. When we suffer for the gospel, we are not alone. As Peter and Paul would tell us, the worst they can do is kill us—and once that's over, we'll be in the presence of our Lord.

That's why Paul, in 2 Timothy 1:9–10, says to Timothy, "This grace was given us in Christ Jesus before the beginning of time, but it has now been revealed through the appearing of our Savior, Christ Jesus, who has destroyed death and has brought life and immortality to light through the gospel." In other words, do not be afraid of death. Why? Because God saved us, called us, and has brought us from death to life. Through His death and resurrection, Jesus has abolished death for all believers.

THREE KINDS OF DEATH

The Bible speaks of death in three different ways. First, there is physical death, in which the soul is separated from the body. Second, there is spiritual death, in which the soul of the nonbeliever is separated from God. Third, there is eternal death, the separation of both body and soul of nonbelievers from God forever and ever.

All three forms of death are the result of sin. All three forms of death are sin's reward. But are you ready for the wonderful news? Are you ready to jump up and shout?

For those who believe in Him, *Jesus has abolished eternal death*!

He has not abolished physical death—even believers die physically. But physical death is a very different experience for the believer than for the nonbeliever. We who have placed our trust in Christ will live forever with Him. Though we all die physically, the believer has the authority to taunt and mock death, as Paul himself wrote, "Where, O death, is your victory? Where, O death, is your sting?" (1 Cor. 15:55).

The grim specter of death, which has haunted humanity since Adam and Eve were cast out of Eden, holds no terror for those who belong to Jesus. After Lazarus died and was laid in the tomb, Jesus said to Martha, the sister of Lazarus, "I am the resurrection and the life. The one who believes in me will live, even though they die; and whoever lives by believing in me will never die" (John 11:25–26). Jesus is saying that those who put their trust in Him shall:

- never die;
- never be separated from Him;
- never experience the second death; and
- live forever in the presence of the Lord.

Because of this truth, Paul could say to Timothy, "My spiritual son, what are you afraid of? The worst they can do is kill you. And that is not the end of life. That is not the end of the world. That is the beginning!" Paul, writing from a Roman dungeon, is telling Timothy, "The reason I have victory in this prison, the reason I have victory in the final days before my execution, the reason I am *not* afraid of what they can do to me, the reason I am *not* ashamed of the gospel, no matter how much opposition or persecution I face is because I know I have already passed from death to life. I know that, whether my physical body is dead or alive, I am already seated in the heavenly realms with my Lord and Savior, Jesus Christ." (See Ephesians 2:6.)

Look again at Paul's resounding message to Timothy in verses 9 and 10:

> This grace was given us in Christ Jesus before the beginning of time, but it has now been revealed through the appearing of our Savior, Christ Jesus, who has destroyed death and has brought life and immortality to light through the gospel.

From before the beginning of time, God had a plan of grace and salvation for all humanity, and when Jesus Christ appeared, that grace was fully revealed. Jesus destroyed death and brought eternal life to light. And please understand, the eternal life Jesus gives us is life forever and ever in a glorified physical body.

Many people, including many Christians, do not understand what the Bible teaches about our eternal life with Him. Many have been fooled by ridiculous images in movies and cartoons that depict heaven as a place where we sit on clouds, strumming harps and wearing halos and angel wings. Nothing could be further from the truth.

The moment we die, we go immediately into the presence of the Lord and receive our glorified bodies. As Jesus told the repentant thief on the cross, "Truly I tell you, today you will be with me in paradise" (Luke 23:43). And as Paul wrote, "For the perishable must clothe itself with the imperishable, and the mortal with immortality" (1 Cor. 15:53).

"But our citizenship is in heaven," writes Paul. "And we eagerly await a Savior from there, the Lord Jesus Christ, who, by the power that enables him to bring everything under his control, will transform our lowly bodies so that they will be like his glorious body" (Phil. 3:20–21). When this body gives up on me, I have a superior physical and supernatural body ready for me.

You may not face imprisonment and beheading like Paul, but you may have to pay a price for taking an uncompromising stand for God's truth. You may be passed over for promotion. You may lose an important business deal. You may be snubbed and persecuted by people you once thought of as friends. You may be suspended or fired from your job. As the world grows increasingly more hostile toward Jesus and His followers, you may even lose your life for the sake of the gospel.

For the believer, the only consequence of death is that you move from the basement to the penthouse. It will be a day of rejoicing and blessing.

THE HOSTILITY OF THIS WORLD

Have you ever wondered why nonbelievers display such an intense hatred for Jesus and His followers? What is it about our faith in God's infallible Word that triggers such hostility among the unsaved? The answer may be simpler than you think.

The gospel tells us that we are lost in our sin, and there is no way we can save ourselves through good works. Salvation is by grace through faith, not of works (Eph. 2:8–9). The moment we recognize the awfulness of our sin and cast ourselves upon God's mercy and grace, He forgives, transforms, and justifies us. That is the gospel message.

That message is a problem for nonbelievers because the natural human mind cannot admit the gravity and horror of sin. The natural mind says, "I admit I'm not perfect, but I'm a good person. If there is a God, He will accept me. I don't need a Savior. So keep your 'sin' talk to yourself. Don't bother me with your gospel."

The natural mind refuses to admit to having sinned so grievously that Jesus would have to die. "You're telling me Jesus died to save me? *Me?* Are you calling *me* a hopeless, helpless sinner? How dare you!"

That's why in church after church preachers have stopped preaching the gospel of redemption from sin and now preach a message of human virtue. They have stopped preaching the cross and the empty tomb and instead preach positive thinking. They have stopped preaching justification by grace through faith and instead preach social justice propaganda.

These preachers want to be liked and admired by nonbelievers. They want to have a popular ministry that rakes in big donations from people who only attend church to have their egos flattered.

What did Paul tell Timothy to do in a world that is hostile to the gospel of salvation? And what are we to do? Answer: guard the truth!

> What you heard from me, keep as the pattern of sound teaching, with faith and love in Christ Jesus. Guard the good deposit that was entrusted to you—guard it with the help of the Holy Spirit who lives in us.
>
> —2 TIMOTHY 1:13–14

The "pattern of sound teaching" Paul writes of is *God's blueprint.* The word translated "pattern" is the same word used for an architectural design. What happens if a builder decides to ignore the architectural blueprint? What if the builder decides he doesn't want to bother putting up the pillars, crossbeams, and archways that are specified by the architect? The building will collapse.

The Word of God is our blueprint for the church and for the Christian life. Many so-called Christian leaders today have cast aside the blueprint for the church. They think they can build on a foundation of worldly ideologies, but the collapse is coming. It's unavoidable. Their churches will collapse, their families will collapse, and their lives will collapse.

If we, as the church, cast aside God's blueprint—the uncompromised Word of God—then the church will cease to be the church of Jesus Christ. Sooner or later, our appetite for God's Word will wane. Sooner or later, spiritual starvation will set in. Sooner or later, a desire for spiritual fellowship will wither. Sooner or later, a critical and divisive spirit will set in. The church will be nothing but a collection of selfish, ambitious egos striving for dominance. And like a house of cards, it will come tumbling down.

And that is why the apostle Paul, in the closing days of his life, pleads with Timothy—and with you and me—to please, please, please follow the blueprint of sound teaching. Please, please, please guard the deposit of truth that was entrusted to you. Don't try to improve on it. Don't deviate from it. Don't modify it.

Above all, don't *ever* grow weary of upholding God's truth. Regardless of opposition, persecution, suffering, or personal cost, follow the blueprint and guard the truth. Never be ashamed of the gospel.

FALSE TEACHERS
IN THE CHURCH

As you read through Paul's second and final letter to Timothy, it becomes clear that he carries a great emotional burden in the closing days of his life. What is this burden? False teachers had infiltrated the church.

False teachers are widespread in the twenty-first-century church, and they were already widespread in the first-century church.

Some false teachers pervert the gospel for their own enrichment. They have greedy, selfish motives, and their god is the almighty dollar. Other false teachers have "good intentions." Their "gospel" is one of improving society and treating people fairly and making sure that no one's feelings are hurt by talk of sin or judgment.

But whether their motive is greed or good intentions, they have corrupted the gospel. They are robbing the church of the priceless treasure of truth that the Lord has entrusted to His church.

Though Paul is burdened by the subversion of the church, he is able to say, "That is why I am suffering as I am. Yet this is no cause for shame, because I know whom I have believed, and am convinced that he is able to guard what I have entrusted to him until that day" (2 Tim. 1:12). What day? The day of the Lord's return!

As Paul faces death, he knows Timothy will be an instrument for preserving the truth of the gospel. At the same time, Paul is aware of Timothy's tendency of discouragement, fear, and timidity. So Paul tells Timothy he does not have to carry this burden alone. Though the church has been infiltrated by false teachers, Timothy can rely on God to guard His truth until the Lord's return.

In the closing lines of this chapter, we see that many in the first-century church have defected from the truth. Paul names two individuals in particular: Phygelus and Hermogenes. They couldn't stand up to persecution, so they fell away (v. 15).

Paul also expresses gratitude for those who stood firm for the truth, especially a faithful Christian named Onesiphorus (vv. 16–18). The Bible tells us little about Onesiphorus (who is not to be confused with Onesimus, the slave mentioned in Paul's letter to Philemon). Ancient tradition suggests that Onesiphorus may have been one of the seventy-two disciples sent out by Jesus to preach. (See Luke 10). Though Phygelus and Hermogenes defected, Onesiphorus remained faithful.

Today Christians around the world suffer persecution, torture, and death for the sake of Jesus Christ. Christians in America are not persecuted to that extent—not yet. But many who call themselves Christians are abandoning the gospel out of mere embarrassment and shame. They don't want to face ridicule from their worldly friends, so they sell out the gospel and conform to this fallen world.

Others, trying to live in peaceful coexistence with this fallen world, have "deconstructed" their faith (yes, that's the buzzword they use). They toss out the parts of the gospel they consider offensive and try to retain some semblance of Jesus and His teachings—though, of course, everything He said about sin, judgment, hell, His death and resurrection, and His second coming must go. Once they have finished deconstructing the Christian faith, what do they have left?

THE LORD IS TRUSTWORTHY

One popular evangelical author and leader went through this process a few years ago. His name is Joshua Harris. Beginning in the late 1990s, he wrote a series of best-selling books on the Christian view of dating and relationships. By age thirty, he was the pastor of a megachurch in Maryland. In 2018, while in his mid-forties, he publicly disavowed his earlier books. In 2019 he announced he was going through a divorce. He soon followed that announcement with a statement on Instagram, which included these sad words:

> I have undergone a massive shift in regard to my faith in Jesus. The popular phrase for this is "deconstruction," the biblical phrase is "falling away." By all the measurements that I have for defining a Christian, I am not a Christian. Many people tell me that there is a different way to practice faith and I want to remain open to this, but I'm not there now.[5]

I fear for this man. I sincerely pray he will find his way to a biblically grounded faith in Jesus Christ. He diagnosed his own condition with devastating accuracy. He has fallen away from the faith. His story is a sobering lesson to us all.

Like Phygelus and Hermogenes, we all risk falling away from the faith when we become embarrassed by the gospel. We risk falling away when, instead of guarding God's truth, we begin to deconstruct it. We risk falling away when we seek friendship with the world instead of faithfulness to the Lord.

Paul's message to Timothy and to us is keep the pattern of sound teaching and guard the good deposit of truth that was entrusted to you. The Lord is faithful to His Word. He will never allow the light of the gospel to be extinguished. God has entrusted the gospel to us, but He has not abdicated. He is watching over His Word. He will preserve it, with or without us. Whether or not we remain faithful, He will always be faithful.

He is trustworthy. He will accomplish *all* things according to the counsel of His will.

Whatever you are going through, whatever trials and obstacles you face in life, you can trust Jesus, the faithful and true. All He asks is that you be faithful to His Word.

CHAPTER 3

SOLDIERS, FARMERS, AND ATHLETES FOR TRUTH

IN OCTOBER 2019, the UK/USA newsmagazine *The Week* published an opinion piece titled "The Coming End of Christian America." The writer declared:

> America is still a "Christian nation," if the term simply means a majority of the population will claim the label when a pollster calls. But, as a new Pew Research report unsparingly explains, the decline of Christianity in the United States "continues at a rapid pace." A bare 65 percent of Americans now say they're Christians, down from 78 percent as recently as 2007. The deconverted are mostly moving away from religion altogether, and the ranks of the religiously unaffiliated— the "nones"—have swelled from 16 to 26 percent

over the same period. If this rate of change continues, the U.S. will be majority non-Christian by about 2035, with the nones representing well over one-third of the population.[1]

The Christian church exists for the purpose of making disciples and expanding the kingdom. Something is seriously wrong if the church is losing disciples and shrinking the kingdom. Jesus told His disciples, "Go into all the world and preach the gospel to all creation" (Mark 16:15). If we were carrying out that commandment as the church in the twenty-first century, the headline would not be "The Coming End of Christian America," but "The Amazing Revival Across America."

From the first century to the twenty-first, the greatest threat to Christianity has never come from the outside. Our greatest threat has never been persecution. It has never been the opposition of atheists. It has never been attacks from our godless culture. It has never been competition from other religions. In fact, external attacks have always strengthened the church.

The greatest threat to the Christian church has always come from within. It has always come from those who claim to be Christians. It has always come from deceptive leaders within the church who preach falsehood, claiming they are reimagining Christianity and even saving Christianity by undermining its teachings.

DEMONIC CONFUSION

No one understood the grave internal threat to the church better than the apostle Paul. In fact, this internal danger is at the very heart of his final letter to Timothy. Paul understood that defection from God's truth starts with confusion. And who is the god of confusion? Satan. And Satan has been sowing confusion in the church from the beginning to the present day.

Today there is confusion over marriage and the family. Should the church ordain marriage strictly according to the biblical pattern of one man and one woman? Or should the church adopt the world's view, in which marriage might consist of two men or two women or any number of people of assorted genders? I'm not making light of the subject. This is literally a matter of serious discussion in many churches today.

There is confusion over abortion. Some in the church adopt the biblical position, as expressed in such passages as Psalm 139:13–16 and Jeremiah 1:5, that an unborn baby is a human being who deserves to be protected from murder. And Exodus 20:13 makes it clear that murder is a crime against God. Others in the church have adopted the world's view, which is that abortion is a women's health issue and no other point of view (including that of the unborn baby) needs to be considered.

So there is confusion about what is right and what is wrong. There is confusion about sexuality, so-called sexual orientation and gender identity. There is confusion about whether the Word of God should have authority over our lives and over the church. Satan, the god of confusion, is active in the church today. Because of Satan's confusing activity, along with the lack of biblical understanding of many in the church, people throw their hands in the air and exclaim, "I just don't know what to believe anymore!"

That's the moment when Satan and his demons high-five one another and pop champagne corks in the infernal realm. That's yet another victory the forces of hell have won over the church of Jesus Christ.

That's why Paul, in his last will and testament, 2 Timothy, appeals to his young friend and to future church leaders, saying, "Whatever you do, don't give up on biblical truth. Don't fall for satanic confusion. Don't get sidetracked by worldly notions and useless debates. Don't waste your time on people who just want to confuse you."

BE STRONG!

The Word of God is our only true and lasting source of encouragement and joy. Human ideas and human belief systems only bring conflict and confusion. If we want to understand reality from God's point of view, if we want to eliminate confusion from our thinking, we must go to God's Word. And Paul, writing under the inspiration of the Holy Spirit, offers us true encouragement and clear thinking when he writes to Timothy:

You then, my son, be strong in the grace that is in Christ Jesus. And the things you have heard me say in the presence of many witnesses entrust to reliable people who will also be qualified to teach others. Join with me in suffering, like a good soldier of Christ Jesus. No one serving as a soldier gets entangled in civilian affairs, but rather tries to please his commanding officer. Similarly, anyone who competes as an athlete does not receive the victor's crown except by competing according to the rules. The hardworking farmer should be the first to receive a share of the crops. Reflect on what I am saying, for the Lord will give you insight into all this.

Remember Jesus Christ, raised from the dead, descended from David. This is my gospel, for which I am suffering even to the point of being chained like a criminal. But God's word is not chained. Therefore I endure everything for the sake of the elect, that they too may obtain the salvation that is in Christ Jesus, with eternal glory.

Here is a trustworthy saying: If we died with him, we will also live with him; if we endure, we will also reign with him. If we disown him, he will also disown us; if we are faithless, he remains faithful, for he cannot disown himself.

—2 TIMOTHY 2:1–13

Look again at what Paul says in verse 1: "You then, my son, be strong in the grace that is in Christ Jesus." How are we to be strong? By gritting our teeth? By pulling ourselves up by our bootstraps? By statements of self-affirmation, "Yes, I can! Yes, I can!"?

No! The strength Paul speaks of doesn't come from within. We only become strong through the grace that is in Jesus Christ.

The words *be strong* are in the imperative mood in the original Greek, which means Paul is giving Timothy a loving command. It's the kind of command a father would give a son for his own good.

One of the great paradoxes of Scripture is this: our almighty sovereign God chooses to entrust His truth to His fumbling, stumbling adopted children. And because we are fallible human beings, we are incapable of guarding God's truth in our own strength. We can only guard and proclaim this message by the grace that is in Jesus Christ.

We are saved by grace. We are justified by grace. We are sanctified by grace. We are to live every moment of every day by grace. We are empowered to overcome all opponents and opposition in our daily lives by grace. And that grace will sustain us in upholding God's truth.

ENTRUSTING AND INVESTING

Next, Paul opens his heart to Timothy in a revealing way. He writes, "And the things you have heard me say in the presence of many witnesses entrust to reliable people who will also be qualified to teach others" (v. 2). In other words, Timothy can only experience the power of the grace of God when he invests his life and his deposit of truth in other faithful people. Paul urges Timothy to be strong in the grace of Jesus and to teach others to be strong in the same way.

Paul tells Timothy that he is not merely to guard this deposit of truth that has been given to him, but he is to *entrust* this message to reliable people. To *entrust* is to give something to another person for its care and protection. There is also a sense of *investment* in the word *entrust*. When you entrust your life savings to a financial institution, you are not merely leaving your wealth to sit uselessly in a vault. You are investing in that financial institution, and you expect your investment to grow.

Paul is telling Timothy that he should entrust the gospel message to faithful individuals, and he should invest himself in them so the gospel will expand and spread and grow. Paul also knew that as Timothy invested this message in others, he would overcome his tendency toward timidity. If you want to experience victory over timidity, anxiety, fear, and sorrow, invest yourself in others.

Timid, fearful people are usually self-absorbed and self-focused. By investing ourselves in others, we become focused on others, focused outside of ourselves, and we overcome our fear and timidity. Discipling and mentoring another person are the greatest blessings you can give that person—yet it is also the greatest blessing you can receive. It's the ultimate win-win situation because both sides of a mentoring relationship are greatly blessed.

Faith in Christ is like electricity. It cannot fully enter you and empower you until it passes through you to others. That means sharing your faith through witnessing to the people around you. On an even deeper level, it means entrusting the gospel message to faithful individuals and investing yourself in their lives. It means devoting yourself to discipling and mentoring others.

If you fail to pass God's truth along to the next generation, you not only deprive the next generation of the blessing, but you miss out on a profound blessing yourself. So don't miss out! Become a mentor. Become a "discipler." Entrust this life-changing message to faithful men, women, and young people.

TRUE APOSTOLIC SUCCESSION

Are you familiar with the term "apostolic succession"? It refers to the uninterrupted line of church leaders, beginning with the apostles and continued through bishop after bishop to the present day. This view of apostolic succession is held by Roman Catholics, Anglicans, and Eastern Orthodox churches. In the Roman Catholic tradition, the line of popes is believed to stretch back to the apostle Peter. In the Orthodox tradition, the line of patriarchs is believed to be traceable to other apostles. In the Coptic Orthodox Church of Egypt, the pope or patriarch of the church is believed to be the successor to the apostle Mark, who founded the Christian church in Egypt.

The idea of apostolic succession can be illustrated this way: an apostle lays hands on the head of his successor and—*zap!*—the successor is endowed with supernatural authority and power to carry on the work of the apostle. Later, that successor lays hands on the head of his successor and—*zap!*—the next successor is endowed with authority and power. This process goes on, generation by generation, *zap, zap, zap!* In this way, the authority and power of Peter and the other apostles have been handed down in an unbroken succession to the popes and patriarchs today.

You can probably tell I don't have a high opinion of this notion. There is nothing in Scripture to support the idea of apostolic succession. In fact, during the first three hundred years of Christianity, there was no reliable record maintained of any pope succeeding Peter or of any institutional hierarchy.

Of course, the Roman Catholic Church claims there is an unbroken succession from Peter to the present pope. There is even a poster for sale on Amazon called "The Supreme Pontiffs of Rome (33AD–Present)," which purports to show all 266 popes of Catholic history.[2] If you saw that poster, you might think the succession of popes from Peter to the present is settled, well-documented history. But that poster glosses over some serious historical problems.

For example, the second pope, who supposedly

succeeded the apostle Peter, was a man named Linus, according to the Catholic Church. He is alleged to be the same Linus who is mentioned in the closing lines of 2 Timothy: "Eubulus greets you, and so do Pudens, Linus, Claudia and all the brothers and sisters" (2 Tim. 4:21).

That brief mention is all we know about Linus— that he was one of Paul's faithful friends in Rome. Everything else that is claimed about this man, including the claim that he was the second pope, is uncorroborated tradition.

The Catholic Church claims the successor of Linus was a man named Anacletus. So little is known of this man that the date he took office as pope and the date of his death are shrouded in mystery. Today the church claims that Anacletus was also known by the name of Cletus. Yet the *Liber Pontificalis* (*Book of the Popes*) and the fourth-century *Liberian Catalogue* listed Anacletus and Cletus as two separate popes. If the Catholic Church cannot even be sure if one of its earliest popes was one man or two different men, what does that tell us about the reliability of these claims?

I do believe in what I call "true apostolic succession." It is not an unbroken series of popes. It is an unbroken series of genuine believers who guarded the deposit of truth they received. These believers then entrusted the truth to faithful individuals, investing their lives in others so the gospel would spread and grow. The true apostolic succession is summed up by Paul in 2 Timothy 2:2, "And the things you have heard me say in the presence of many witnesses entrust to reliable people who will also be qualified to teach others."

We cannot pass apostolic authority and apostolic power from one person to the next by the laying on of hands. Rather, we entrust the gospel message to the next generation by teaching others who are qualified to teach. We light a torch with God's truth, and with that torch we light another torch, and another, and another. In this way, the light of God's truth spreads throughout the world, turning the night as bright as day.

Friend in Christ, this process of entrusting God's truth to others, of lighting torch after torch after torch, cannot happen when we merely attend church, listen to a sermon, then leave church and go on about our lives. As we are about to see, this all-important process of entrusting God's truth to others only happens when we learn to see ourselves not merely as church members but as soldiers, farmers, and athletes for the gospel.

SOLDIERS FOR THE GOSPEL

In 2 Timothy 2, Paul offers Timothy three word pictures to help him cut through the confusion and focus on what is important: the soldier, the farmer, and the athlete.

Why does Paul begin with the example of a soldier? Paul wants us to understand that the Christian life is spiritual warfare. Soldiers do not expect a soft or easy life. Soldiers take hardship as a matter of course.

Soldiers are ready to take risks, including risking their own lives. Above all, soldiers fight to win.

I have enormous respect for men and women who put on military uniforms and serve their country with honor and courage. And I also have enormous respect for Christian soldiers who go into spiritual battle, risking persecution and their own lives, often taking the gospel behind enemy lines into countries where it is forbidden to witness about the Lord Jesus Christ.

In the spiritual battle, there are only two kinds of people: victims and victors. If you want to be a victor in spiritual warfare, you must learn the rules of the battlefield. To win this war, you cannot watch the battle from the sidelines. You must step out onto the battlefield. You must risk being wounded and bloodied.

Why are secular forces—the atheists in academia, the anti-Christians in the media, and the secularists in government—having so much success in eradicating the biblical worldview from our society? It's because Christians have surrendered the battlefield. Christians have surrendered the public schools, the universities, the halls of government, the entertainment media, the news media, and on and on. When Christians deserted the battlefield, the nonbelievers took over. When Christians surrendered the battlefield of the mainline denominations, the nonbelievers took over.

Wherever there has been a battle for some segment of our society, the nonbelievers have fought for dominance and the Christians have given up and moved away. The hardship was too painful and the conflict too unpleasant, so the Christians ran up the white flag of surrender.

The apostle Paul's message to Timothy and to us is this, "Join with me in suffering, like a good soldier of Christ Jesus. No one serving as a soldier gets entangled in civilian affairs, but rather tries to please his commanding officer" (2 Tim. 2:3–4).

Soldiers of Jesus readily endure suffering and hardship. Soldiers do not get entangled in civilian life—that is, they do not put worldly success, gaining power and fame, being entertained, and other civilian pursuits ahead of serving Jesus. As good soldiers, we don't fall into the trap of pleasing other people. Our one and only goal is pleasing our commander in chief, the Lord Jesus.

ATHLETES FOR THE GOSPEL

Next, Paul uses the image of an athlete to illustrate how we are to faithfully entrust the truth of the gospel to reliable people who will in turn teach others. In verse 5, he writes: "Similarly, anyone who competes as an athlete does not receive the victor's crown except by competing according to the rules."

As spiritual athletes, we do *not* compete against one another. We do *not* try to outperform one another. Our opponent isn't fellow Christians, but the world, the flesh, and the devil.

In ancient Greece, the winning athlete was crowned with an evergreen wreath. To win the wreath, an athlete had to compete according to the rules. A Greek runner could not take a shortcut to the finish line. A Greek javelin thrower could not step over the runway mark while throwing. A Greek discus thrower could not set foot outside the throwing circle. Athletes must compete according to the rules. An athlete who breaks the rules forfeits the evergreen crown.

You and I may not look like athletes; we may not compete in a footrace for an Olympic medal, but we are athletes for Jesus. We are in the race of our lives. We must run our race, *not* according to our own whims and desires, but according to the rules Jesus put in place.

There are many people today, including many within the church, who want to rewrite the rules of the race. They have invented new rules for a reimagined, reinvented Christianity. They have invented new rules for a feel-good Christianity that has no moral judgment, no cross, no talk of sin, no need for repentance, and no hell. They have invented new rules for a prosperity gospel in which we don't serve God, He serves us—and His will for our lives is a mansion with a Mercedes in the driveway.

If you run your race by the wrong set of rules, you'll reach the end of your life and find it has all been wasted. You won't find the rules of the spiritual race in the words of some silver-tongued false preacher. You'll only find the Lord's rules in His Word, the Bible.

FARMERS FOR THE GOSPEL

The next image Paul gives us is that of a hardworking farmer. Farming in Paul's day was backbreaking work. There was no mechanized farm equipment. Tilling the soil in those days was conducted by an ox, a plow, and a very strong man. He would do his job whether the soil was good and rich or hard and rocky. He worked in good weather and bad. He didn't have the luxury of saying, "I don't feel like planting this year. I'd rather take a few weeks off." He didn't have the luxury at harvesttime to say, "I just don't feel like gathering the crop today. I'm going to take a mental health day."

I tip my hat to the farmers of the first century and the twenty-first century. Farmers today have modern conveniences that didn't exist in Paul's day. But farmers still have to work hard, even on days they'd rather be doing something else. The crops won't wait. They must be planted at planting time and harvested at harvesttime.

As the Book of Proverbs warns, "Sluggards [that is, lazy farmers] do not plow in season; so at harvest time they look but find nothing" (Prov. 20:4). And that is why Paul says in 2 Timothy 2:6, "The hardworking farmer should be the first to receive a share of the crops."

Paul is telling us that we need to be very diligent and careful in tilling the soil of our lives and our character. We need to daily sow the seed of the Word of

God into our lives. If we do, we will harvest a crop of holiness and blessing in our lives.

As we sow the seed of God's Word in our lives, we must also till the soil and scatter seed in the lives of those around us: our spouses and children, the people we teach and disciple, the people we mentor in the workplace and on campus, and the people we influence in our neighborhoods. We will not reap a great harvest unless we are sowing the seed of God's Word wherever we go.

Let's summarize: There can be no victory for the soldier who does not fight. There can be no wreath for the athlete who breaks the rules. There can be no harvest for the farmer unless he tills the soil, plants the seed, and gathers the crop at harvesttime.

The Lord Jesus has called us to be soldiers, athletes, and farmers for the gospel. Paul sums this up in verse 7: "Reflect on what I am saying, for the Lord will give you insight into all this."

When you read the Bible, do you reflect on what God is saying to you through His Word? Or do you read the Bible so you can check the box on your to-do list, "Read the Bible today"?

James 1:23–24 tells us, "Anyone who listens to the word but does not do what it says is like someone who looks at his face in a mirror and, after looking at himself, goes away and immediately forgets what he looks like." James is describing someone who reads the Bible without applying its truth to his life. He's describing a person who reads without reflecting and meditating on the Word.

This passage in James reminds us of why we need to pray before reading the Bible. The Holy Spirit who dwells within us is the same Spirit who inspired and authored the Bible. If we will seek the leading and filling of the Holy Spirit, the Spirit will open our eyes to the wonderful treasures in God's Word.

In the early hours of the morning, when I am alone with the Word of God open before me, I quiet my thoughts and meditate on the words God is speaking to my heart. I often hear the Holy Spirit say to me, "This is a word of encouragement for you" or "This is a word of affirmation for you" or "Listen up—this is a rebuke for you" or "This is a challenge for you" or "This is a correction for you."

So Paul's message to Timothy—and to you and me—is, "Reflect on what I am saying, for the Lord will give you insight into all this."

REMEMBER JESUS

In verse 8, Paul takes Timothy back to the basics: "Remember Jesus Christ, raised from the dead, descended from David. This is my gospel."

Remember Jesus? How could Timothy ever forget Jesus? How could you or I ever forget Jesus? Why does Paul even need to say this? Forgetting Jesus would be unthinkable, right?

Unfortunately, no. Believers forget Jesus all the time.

We have fickle memories, distractions, busy schedules, and all too often, we do forget Jesus.

How many times have you found yourself in a challenging situation, facing an unsolvable problem, and you responded with panic, anger, or blame? Did you remember Jesus in that time of crisis? Did you remember to pray? Did you remember to ask for God's wisdom? Did you remember to ask for God's help?

You see, we often forget Jesus just when we need Him most.

When we face an unsolvable problem, our response should not be the classic "deer in the headlights" paralysis. Our response should be an active, prayerful, fully engaged response of faith: "Lord, what do You want me to do? Lord, please give me Your wisdom for this crisis. Lord, help me make the right decision. Lord, help me face this situation with grace and trust in You."

And when you find yourself in conflict—a major argument with your boss, coworker, spouse, or child— are you thinking only of your counterarguments, your defenses, your resentment, and how unfairly you're being treated? In the heat of an angry argument, do you let your emotions take over? Or do you remember Jesus?

Jesus taught that "anyone who is angry with a brother or sister will be subject to judgment" and is unworthy to offer a gift to God at the altar until the matter is resolved (Matt. 5:21–24). Jesus also said, "Love your enemies, do good to those who hate you, bless those who curse you, pray for those who mistreat you. If someone slaps you on one cheek, turn to them the other also. If someone takes your coat, do not withhold your shirt from them" (Luke 6:27–29).

Paul tells Timothy, "Remember Jesus Christ, raised from the dead, descended from David." Remember Jesus because the gospel is all about Him. Remember Jesus because He is our great example and role model. Remember Jesus because the Holy Spirit can enable the love of Jesus to shine through us. Remember Jesus because God the Father raised Him from the dead. Remember Jesus because, as the son of David, He is human like us, even though He is also God in human form.

Remember Jesus, who died on the cross—but did not stay on the cross. Remember Jesus, who was buried in the tomb—but did not stay in the tomb. Remember Jesus, whose Good Friday was followed by Easter Sunday. Remember Jesus, who wept in the garden of Gethsemane—but turned Mary Magdalene's weeping to joy in the garden of the resurrection.

"Remember Jesus," Paul said to Timothy.

"Remember Jesus," Paul still says to you and me.

Remember Jesus as you are soldiering for the gospel.

Remember Jesus as you compete as an athlete for the gospel.

Remember Jesus as you labor as a good farmer for the gospel.

Remember Jesus as you battle temptation by God's power. Remember His suffering on the cross as you endure pain and persecution. Remember that your suffering is only for a season and will not last forever.

Paul is saying to us, "Remember Jesus, because the time is coming when there will be no more tears, and the heavy weight of sin and sorrow will fall away and be no more."

Let's build a habit, in both the good and hard times, of remembering Jesus, of thanking Jesus, of patterning our lives after Jesus, and of looking forward to the return of Jesus.

That is Paul's gospel. That is our gospel. And that is our hope.

LET TODAY BE THE DAY

In the closing lines of 2 Timothy 2, Paul contrasts the chains of his imprisonment with the power of God's unchained Word: "This is my gospel, for which I am suffering even to the point of being chained like a criminal. But God's word is not chained. Therefore I endure everything for the sake of the elect, that they too may obtain the salvation that is in Christ Jesus, with eternal glory" (2 Tim. 2:8–10).

Paul is confined to a dungeon cell. Nothing confines or restrains God's Word. Paul willingly endures the chains and suffering of a Roman prison so others may hear God's unchained Word and be saved.

The apostle concludes this section by quoting the lines from a great hymn of the early church:

> Here is a trustworthy saying: If we died with
> him, we will also live with him; if we endure,
> we will also reign with him. If we disown him,
> he will also disown us; if we are faithless, he
> remains faithful, for he cannot disown himself.
>   —2 TIMOTHY 2:11–13

If we die with Jesus—if we die to self, if we die to sin, and even if we die by the executioner's axe—we shall live forever with Him. If we endure suffering and persecution, we shall reign and rule with Him. If we persevere and stand our biblical ground, if we refuse to surrender in this epic spiritual battle, He will honor and reward us as soldiers of the gospel. If we deny Him, He will deny us. If we are unfaithful to the gospel, He will still remain faithful—and He will see that the gospel goes out to all nations, even if we fall away. Though unfaithfulness is an all-too-human trait in us, faithfulness is the essence of God's nature.

Today there are people who preach a false gospel called "hyper grace." This false gospel claims you can practice sin to your heart's content, and you need not confess, repent, or worry about your sin. The hyper grace of God will cover it.

The people who teach this false gospel have twisted verse 13 to rationalize this evil doctrine: "If we are faithless, he remains faithful, for he cannot disown himself." The hyper grace false teachers claim this as their license to sin.

They claim that Paul is saying, in effect, "If we are

faithless, God will still remain faithful to us and let our sins slide because He cannot disown Himself." Nothing could be further from the truth! Paul is really saying that if we are unfaithful to God, God will remain faithful to His promises. And what are His promises? He has promised He will deny the unfaithful.

The International Standard Version renders it this way: "Our faith may fail, his never wanes—that's who he is, he cannot change!"

In other words, God will do all things in a manner consistent with who He is. He offers us salvation by grace through faith, and if we put our faith in Him, He will save us because that is who God is and He cannot change. But if we choose to live a life of sin and refuse to live by faith in Him, then *He will deny us* because we do not have a saving faith.

Hyper grace is one of Satan's cleverest lies. Satan takes a verse of Scripture—a profound statement of truth about God—and distorts it into an evil doctrine designed to destroy human souls.

Some false teachers claim that, in the end, God will feel sorry for all people, and He will open the gates of heaven and let everybody in. Again, that is a satanic lie. For God to set aside His free plan of salvation, set aside the judgment of sin, and let unrepentant sinners climb over the walls of heaven instead of coming through the narrow gate—that would be contrary to who He is.

God's faithfulness is demonstrated in both His love *and* His justice. His love says, "Come to Me through

A WORKER WHO IS UNASHAMED

The evidence of satanic activity is everywhere in the world, but people are blind to Satan's presence because they are convinced he doesn't exist. Only those who are spiritually aware of the reality of the devil can see that he is active in our world.

Satan is committed to obliterating God's truth and replacing it with falsehood. This has been Satan's goal ever since he and his demons fell from heaven. We have seen Satan's assault on God's truth down through the centuries and in our own lifetime. Churches that once championed God's inerrant Word have completely abandoned God's Word today. Colleges and universities that were founded as centers of Christian learning by Bible-believing people—Oxford, Harvard, Yale, and Princeton, to name a few—have become citadels of atheism and aggressive hostility toward God's Word.

No one other than Jesus has understood the deceptions of Satan better than the apostle Paul. That is why, in the second half of 2 Timothy 2, Paul writes:

> Keep reminding God's people of these things. Warn them before God against quarreling about words; it is of no value, and only ruins those who listen. Do your best to present yourself to God as one approved, a worker who does not need to be ashamed and who correctly handles the word of truth. Avoid godless chatter, because

those who indulge in it will become more and more ungodly. Their teaching will spread like gangrene. Among them are Hymenaeus and Philetus, who have departed from the truth. They say that the resurrection has already taken place, and they destroy the faith of some. Nevertheless, God's solid foundation stands firm, sealed with this inscription: "The Lord knows those who are his," and, "Everyone who confesses the name of the Lord must turn away from wickedness."

In a large house there are articles not only of gold and silver, but also of wood and clay; some are for special purposes and some for common use. Those who cleanse themselves from the latter will be instruments for special purposes, made holy, useful to the Master and prepared to do any good work.

Flee the evil desires of youth and pursue righteousness, faith, love and peace, along with those who call on the Lord out of a pure heart. Don't have anything to do with foolish and stupid arguments, because you know they produce quarrels. And the Lord's servant must not be quarrelsome but must be kind to everyone, able to teach, not resentful. Opponents must be gently instructed, in the hope that God will grant them repentance leading them to a knowledge of the truth, and that they will come to their senses and escape from the trap of the devil, who has taken them captive to do his will.

—2 Timothy 2:14–26

In the first half of this chapter, Paul gave us three word pictures to show how we are to guard God's truth: the images of a soldier, an athlete, and a farmer. Here, Paul gives us three more word pictures to encourage us in our faithful service: the good worker who is not ashamed, a clean vessel that is fit for honorable use, and the good servant who is obedient, not quarrelsome.

Paul writes, "Keep reminding God's people of these things. Warn them before God against quarreling about words; it is of no value, and only ruins those who listen. Do your best to present yourself to God as one approved, a worker who does not need to be ashamed and who correctly handles the word of truth" (vv. 14–15).

Our motive for living the Christian life is not to please others or to please ourselves. We live to please the Lord. Our goal is to present ourselves to God and receive His approval as workers who have nothing to be ashamed of.

Who *should* be ashamed? False teachers and false preachers who distort and corrupt God's truth out of selfish motives. False teachers have every reason to be ashamed, yet most seem absolutely shameless and even proud of how they have perverted the gospel.

And though Paul's words in this passage are aimed primarily at people in Timothy's position—church leaders, teachers, and preachers—Paul's counsel also applies in a general sense to all Christians. All ministry must be done for the glory of Jesus alone. This is true whether you are leading a church, teaching a

Sunday school class or home Bible study, witnessing to your next-door neighbor, or ladling soup in a homeless shelter. All service to God and others should be done for the glory of Jesus alone. There must be no hidden agenda, no desire for personal gain, and no secret manipulation.

If we purify our motives for serving the Lord, we will eliminate any temptation to dress up the gospel to make it more palatable to the world. We will eliminate any temptation to disguise the gospel with some worldly marketing program. We will preach, teach, and share the uncompromised gospel of Jesus Christ in plain, straightforward terms.

TO LOVE OTHERS, LOVE THE TRUTH

In 1992 I received a letter from a young woman who listened to our radio show (this was before we were on television). She wrote, "I have become a Christian after listening to the gospel on your radio show. I have felt convicted about living with my boyfriend. So I went to him and said, 'I can no longer sleep with you unless we are married.' When I said that, he became angry. My ultimatum brought out all the negative feelings he had about Christianity."

I was a much younger pastor then, and I confess I was not as guarded in my speech as I am today. So I gave her some very straightforward advice: "What you said to him is exactly right. His anger toward

Christianity is his problem, not yours. You need to dump the fool."

Now, if I received the same letter today, I would not use the word *fool*, but I would give her the same advice. She knew what the gospel demanded of her. She knew the right thing to do. She just wanted to have the urging of the Spirit within her confirmed.

The Word of God is always clear. The Word of God is always straight. The Word of God is always plain. And Paul is telling us to keep it that way. There should be no silly quarreling about this word or that word. Let's teach God's Word plainly and correctly. Let's apply it to our lives in a straightforward way.

Not everyone who hears God's Word will accept His message. Not everyone who hears will open their hearts and be saved. But we must continue to love others and preach the uncompromised truth. Some who compromise God's truth will claim they are doing so out of love, making statements like, "I don't want to offend people with talk of sin, judgment, and hell, so I'm only going to tell people about the love of God."

You cannot truly love people with the love of God while withholding the truth of God. Those who corrupt God's truth out of a misplaced notion of loving others are only being self-centered. They are trying to spare themselves the confrontation, the tough questions, and the hostility of people who don't want to hear about sin and judgment. They are not trying to spare the feelings of others. They are trying to make themselves more popular with the world.

Those who speak God's uncompromised truth risk being rejected and persecuted. Yet that is what God calls us to endure for the sake of the gospel. If we refuse to compromise the gospel, we can one day stand before God as workers who need not be ashamed because we have correctly handled the Word of truth.

Paul writes, "Warn them before God against quarreling about words; it is of no value, and only ruins those who listen" (v. 14). In other words, do not get drawn into pointless arguments over matters that have been settled in the Word of God. These arguments can actually *ruin* lives, and Paul uses an exceptionally strong word to make this point. The Greek word for *ruin* is *katastrophē*, from which we get the English word *catastrophe*.

Paul is telling us that arguing with one another can ruin Christian friendships, Christian behavior, and even a person's faith. Arguments lead to ungodliness and division in the church, which can spread with catastrophic results.

GODLESS CHATTER

France's King Louis XIV was known as the "Sun King." He ruled during a period of unprecedented power, splendor, and prosperity in France. He lived amid the opulence and luxury of the Palace of Versailles. But on September 1, 1715, just four days short of his seventy-seventh birthday, King Louis XIV died after gangrene infected his leg and spread to his vital organs.

Gangrene is the corruption of body tissue caused by a lack of blood flow that spreads quickly and frequently leads to death.

Paul uses the image of gangrene to warn Timothy—and us—against a poisonous threat to the church. "Avoid godless chatter," Paul writes, "because those who indulge in it will become more and more ungodly. Their teaching will spread like gangrene" (vv. 16–17).

Godless chatter is infectious. It is deadly to the church, the body of Christ, and it spreads quickly, like gangrene. Satan's lies often spread faster than God's truth. Why? Because the sinful human heart is more receptive to the oily, slippery lies of Satan than to God's uncompromised truth.

Paul warns Timothy of two specific people, Hymenaeus and Philetus. Hymenaeus was named after Hymen, the Greek god of marriage (the name comes from an ancient root word meaning "to bind together"). His name conveyed a sense of togetherness and unity. Paul also warned against Hymenaeus in his previous letter, in 1 Timothy 1:20. The name Philetus comes from the Greek verb *phileo*, meaning "to love" someone or something.

These two heretical teachers, whose names suggested unity and love, were anything *but* unifying and loving influences in the early church. They opposed Paul and taught people that there was no future resurrection to look forward to. They taught that it had already passed. You can imagine how you would feel if a "Christian" teacher began teaching that there is no resurrection, no second coming of Christ, but only the grave. It would destroy your hope and faith.

And that is exactly what happened as Hymenaeus and Philetus went from church to church, claiming to represent the gospel of Jesus Christ while preaching that there was no point in following Christ. Their teaching and preaching destroyed the hope of the resurrection for untold numbers of early Christians.

Hymenaeus and Philetus were undoubtedly gifted communicators who made an excellent impression. Deceivers are often very attractive people. They gain our trust through their good looks, their charm, and their eloquence. Like the devil himself, they can be very persuasive.

Twenty-first-century Christianity has been infiltrated with hundreds of such people. They say such things as, "God is love. Therefore, any kind of love is a good thing." If you are not very perceptive, this can sound like a reasonable argument. The catch is that God's love, which the Greek Bible calls *agape*, should never be confused with what these false teachers mean by "love," which is usually some form of sexual behavior.

They say, "Don't get hung up on doctrine." Translation: "Don't tell me what the Bible says. I really don't care."

Or they say, "I follow the sayings of Jesus. I don't believe all the supernatural parts of the gospel." Translation: "I don't believe Jesus is the Son of God. I don't believe in the virgin birth, the miracles, or the resurrection. I just want to pick and choose the teachings of Jesus that appeal to me and don't challenge my thinking."

Or they say, "I believe a lot of the same things that are in the Bible. I just have some additional beliefs, such as reincarnation, karma, and mantra meditation." Translation: "I take a grain of biblical truth, wrap it in some poisonous ideas, sugarcoat it, and call it a new kind of Christianity."

Paul says, "Avoid godless chatter, because those who indulge in it will become more and more ungodly" (v. 16). The more they chatter, the more ungodly their ideas and actions become. Paul is not saying we should avoid nonbelievers. We should have many non-Christian friends and neighbors in our circles of influence, but we should minister to them and share Christ with them every day. We should not allow them to infect our thinking with their worldly ideas.

Paul is saying we should avoid getting caught up in confusing, pointless arguments with false teachers and false believers. They will try to lead you away from sound biblical doctrine. When it becomes clear that they are trying to persuade you to buy into their deceptive notions, don't give them the time of day. Don't listen to their godless chatter.

In verse 19, Paul writes, "Nevertheless, God's solid foundation stands firm, sealed with this inscription: 'The Lord knows those who are his,' and, 'Everyone who confesses the name of the Lord must turn away from wickedness.'"

I believe when Paul writes "The Lord knows those

who are his," he is referring to an incident from the Old Testament. It took place in Numbers 16. There, a man named Korah and more than 250 Israelite men rebelled against Moses and against God. Moses told Korah and his followers, "In the morning the LORD will show who belongs to him and who is holy" (v. 5). And he instructed Korah and his followers to perform a ceremony before the Lord with burning coals and incense. The Lord caused the ground to split apart, and Korah, along with his household, fell into the realm of the dead, and the earth closed over them. And Korah's 250 men were slain as well.

In a stunning display of holy judgment, the Lord demonstrated who among the Israelites were His and who were not.

HOLY AND USEFUL
TO THE MASTER

Next, Paul draws a word picture of a clean utensil that is set apart for the Master's use. He writes, "In a large house there are articles not only of gold and silver, but also of wood and clay; some are for special purposes and some for common use. Those who cleanse themselves from the latter will be instruments for special purposes, made holy, useful to the Master and prepared to do any good work" (2 Tim. 2:20–21).

What is the "large house" Paul refers to? It is the church of Jesus Christ. What are the utensils, pots, and pans in this large house? They are the people who make up the church. In the real world, household utensils don't get to choose whether they will be silver spoons or dirty buckets. But in Paul's word picture, household utensils are able to cleanse themselves for the Master's use.

The Master of the house proudly uses and displays some of the utensils—while others He hides in the basement. People who are faithful to the Lord and His Word are instruments of honor. Those who twist God's truth and teach false ideas are instruments of dishonor and are useless. Those who cleanse themselves, Paul tells us, will be instruments for God's own special purposes. They will be made holy and useful to the Lord, ready to do any good work.

There can be no higher honor in life than to be an instrument in the hand of God. There can be no greater accomplishment in life than to be used to accomplish God's purpose.

But there is a condition for serving God. What is that condition? Cleanliness and purity. This does not mean we must be absolutely perfect. True perfection does not exist, except in heaven. But Paul tells us that we can purify ourselves for God's service. How? By confession and repentance from sin. By dealing squarely with our sin instead of rationalizing it away. By purging our hearts of all false teaching and refusing to listen to false teaching. False teaching is all around us. The following are some examples in our society today:

- "The Bible is not relevant today; it's just a collection of ancient myths and sayings."

- "A loving God would never send anyone to hell."

- "I can believe God might annihilate unrepentant sinners, but He would never condemn anyone to eternal punishment."

- "God gave us the gift of sexuality. He certainly won't condemn me for using it any way I choose."

- "This is my money. I earned it. I'll spend it on myself, and from time to time I'll leave God a tip in the offering plate."

These false ideas are rampant in the church today. If we want to be fit utensils for God's use, we must purify ourselves of all false ideas. We must bathe ourselves daily in the truth of God's Word.

FLEE TEMPTATION, RESIST THE DEVIL

Next, Paul urges Timothy, "Flee the evil desires of youth and pursue righteousness, faith, love and peace, along with those who call on the Lord out of a pure heart" (v. 22).

When you read these words, you undoubtedly think of immoral sexual activity. That is certainly part of what Paul has in mind, but there's more to Paul's counsel than sexual temptation. "The evil desires of youth" also include the common youthful tendency toward self-indulgence, stubbornness, rebellion, arrogance, and a know-it-all attitude. Especially in adolescent years, young people are prone to think they have it all figured out, and they are smarter than their parents, teachers, and other grown-ups. These tendencies in the young come from having so little life experience that they don't know how much they don't know.

We need to understand that the evil desires of youth are not confined to any age group. Though unhealthy sexual desires, headstrong attitudes, and arrogance seem especially rampant among young people, we see these same traits in much older people as well. Whatever our age, Paul pleads with us, "Flee the evil desires of youth and pursue righteousness, faith, love and peace." Don't flirt with temptation; flee as fast as you can.

It might seem that Paul's counsel conflicts with the counsel of James 4:7: "Resist the devil, and he will flee from you." Paul is telling us to flee. James is telling us to resist—and the devil will flee. But these two passages of Scripture are perfectly harmonized and balanced. We are to flee temptation and resist the devil.

Many Christians fall to temptation because they mix up this counsel from God. They try to resist temptation and flee from the devil. When you try to resist temptation instead of fleeing from it, you are really flirting with it. To flee temptation, you must remove temptation from your sight and your mind.

Unfortunately, many believers linger in the presence of temptation. They linger the same way Lot lingered too long in Sodom. (See Genesis 19.) Instead, they should flee temptation the way Joseph fled from Potiphar's wife. (See Genesis 39.)

When you flee temptation, you should not just run away. Instead, you should *run toward righteousness*. Turn your back on the old nature and run to the new. Crucify the flesh and walk in the Spirit. Reject sin and pursue righteousness. That's the secret to godly living.

And how do we resist the devil? Never turn tail and run. With the devil, you must stand your ground. As a believer, you have authority over the devil. He is a defeated foe. He is a toothless lion with no claws. He has no authority over you. He can never separate you from the love of Christ because you have been redeemed by the blood of Jesus on the cross.

So stand up to the devil. Quote Scripture to the devil. Tell him his taunts and accusations have no power over you. Resist him and he will flee.

AVOID TRAPS

Sam Ayoub was an Egyptian-born financier and long-time chief financial officer of the Coca-Cola Company. A founding trustee of The Church of The Apostles, Sam was truly like a father to me. He told me a story about his friend Robert Winship Woodruff, who was president of The Coca-Cola Company from 1923 to 1955.

Woodruff was known to his associates as The Boss. During World War II, Woodruff befriended General Dwight Eisenhower, the supreme commander of Allied forces, who helped Woodruff set up dozens of Coca-Cola bottling plants in Europe, Asia, and North Africa to provide soft drinks to the troops. After Eisenhower became president of the United States in 1953, one of his favorite getaways was Woodruff's Ichauway Plantation in southwest Georgia.

During one of President Eisenhower's overnight stays at Ichauway, he arose bright and early and went downstairs for breakfast. Eisenhower was an early riser, but Mr. Woodruff was not. The house was quiet and empty, and the president of the United States was hungry.

Eisenhower went to the dining room and noticed a bell on the table, so he picked it up, rang it, and then sat in the chair at the head of the table.

Moments later, the chief steward appeared and said, "Yes, sir?"

President Eisenhower said, "I would like some breakfast, please."

"Sir," the chief steward replied, "breakfast is served only when The Boss comes down. Furthermore, you are sitting in his chair."

Those are the words of a faithful, obedient servant. Even though the chief steward was speaking to the president of the United States, his loyalty was to The Boss.

We should keep this scene in mind as we examine the third and final word picture Paul presents to us—the image of an obedient servant. In 2 Timothy 2:24, Paul writes, "And the Lord's servant must not be quarrelsome but must be kind to everyone, able to teach, not resentful."

Just as the hard worker was not ashamed, just as the utensil was clean for the Master's use, the servant is always obedient, kind, an able teacher, and even-tempered. The servant does the Master's will, not his own. Obedience is the servant's single overriding duty. It doesn't matter whether the servant agrees with the Master. He must carry out the Master's will with loyalty and obedience.

Satan tries to entrap us and seduce us into disobedience. Paul writes, in verses 25 and 26, "Opponents must be gently instructed, in the hope that God will grant them repentance leading them to a knowledge of the truth, and that they will come to their senses and escape from the trap of the devil, who has taken them captive to do his will."

In the church, there are obedient servants and there are opponents—people who, out of ignorance or rebellion, set themselves in opposition to God's truth. Paul's counsel to Timothy is that these opponents should be instructed—gently, through persuasion, not harshly through coercion. The goal is to help these opponents come to their senses. While they stand in opposition to God's truth, they are captives of Satan, caught in his trap and fooled into doing his will.

How can we escape Satan's trap? By serving God's truth with joy and gratitude. As God's servants, we must steer clear of Satan's traps and help free others from his traps as well.

One of the traps of the devil I have avoided for many years is the trap of debating nonbelievers. I have received countless invitations to debate prominent atheists and apostates. I turned them all down flat. Why? Because I knew they were invitations to a trap.

The goal of these traps was to get me to place biblical truth on the same level as the opponent's philosophical views. These debates are usually exercises in polemics—rhetorical attacks, mockery, and clever deception—not a fair and honest exchange of facts and logic. These public debates seldom change minds and hearts. They are Satan's traps, and I won't go there.

THE MANSION WE ARE BUILDING

Some time ago I heard a story that is said to be true, and which I have never forgotten. A wealthy building contractor decided to retire after forty years. He said to his foreman, "You've been with me for many years. Let's go out on a high note. As my last project, I want to build the biggest, most lavish mansion we've ever built. The budget for this project is unlimited. I want you to spare no expense and use only the finest materials. I'm going to Europe for a year, so you'll be in charge."

The foreman saw an opportunity to make a dishonest fortune for himself. After the contractor left for Europe, the foreman proceeded to build a mansion out of the cheapest, lowest-grade materials he could find. He charged the company for expensive, high-quality materials and pocketed the difference. No one would ever know.

When the contractor returned from Europe, he met the foreman for an inspection tour of the house. The exterior was beautiful and impressive. As they walked through the house, the contractor said, "How do you like this house you built?"

The foreman said, "I'm very proud of it. It's a fine house! Here are the keys."

The contractor said, "Oh, you keep the keys. This house is my gift to you for all your years of service."

Friend in Christ, you and I are workers building a house. We are the utensils in the house. We are the servants of the Master of the house. Whether we live in contempt or in contentment, in peace or in pain, in depression or in delight, this is the house we are building. It is our house.

Are we *faithful* servants who need not be ashamed? Are we investing in others, as He commands? Are we building this house out of the best materials? Are we furnishing this house with clean, honorable utensils that are fit for the Master's use?

We will spend eternity in the mansion we are building right now as servants of the Master. Let's build with only the best materials and the finest workmanship. Let's build in obedience to Jesus the Master.

CHAPTER 5

THE LAST DAYS

IN 1989 CALIFORNIA congressman William Danne-meyer released a book titled *Shadow in the Land: Homosexuality in America*. Dannemeyer made a series of startling predictions:

> It is quite possible that under new legislation homosexuals will be permitted to marry. At that point, they will then have the legal right to be considered equally and without prejudice when applying to adopt children, something that even a gay rights advocate like Michael Dukakis opposes....Adoption agencies will have no choice in the matter.
>
> Speaking of children, school curricula will have to be revised where they are not already depicting sodomy as normal and a practice acceptable to society. Teachers will have to be hired with an eye toward "sexual orientation," making certain that enough deviates are on the faculty to provide potentially homosexual youths with "role models."

Extracurricular activities will also have to reflect the new status of homosexuality under the law. There will be homosexual clubs in every school...and speakers will be invited to campus to talk to assemblies about the virtues of the homosexual life.

Of course, religious institutions will not be exempt....Even church schools whose students receive government loans will have to hire homosexuals on their faculties and subsidize homosexual activities on campus....

These legal changes...would stand the Judeo-Christian Tradition of 3,000 years on its head.[1]

At the time the book was published, critics called it alarmist and exaggerated because Dannemeyer predicted a series of social changes so extreme that they couldn't possibly happen in America.

Yet they did.

Nearly all Dannemeyer's predictions have come true: same-sex marriage; adoptions by same-sex couples; sex-ed curricula in our schools that normalize not only homosexuality, but bisexuality, transgender, and other sexual orientations and identities; and Gay-Straight Alliance clubs on middle school and high school campuses nationwide.

And what about Dannemeyer's claim that "religious institutions will not be exempt"? On June 15, 2020, the Supreme Court of the United States ruled that Title VII of the 1964 Civil Rights Act protects gay and transgender employees from job discrimination—and it's unclear whether religious schools will be forced to comply. What *is* clear is that federal and state officials across America want to force religious institutions to hire gay and transgender employees, just as Dannemeyer predicted.

I read that book when it first came out, and I heard the critics who said Dannemeyer's predictions would never come to pass. But I knew better. I thought, "Nothing in this book surprises me. I expect all of these predictions to come true." After all, two thousand years ago the apostle Paul predicted the last days would be difficult times for believers.

PAUL'S PROPHECY

In 1973 computer pioneer Jay Forrester of MIT developed a program called World One. Forrester had been commissioned to create the program by the Club of Rome, a hundred-member group of government leaders, UN officials, economists, and business leaders from around the world. The Club of Rome wanted to ensure that human civilization would be sustainable in the future.

World One analyzed the complex interactions of population growth, economic and political trends, the scarcity of natural resources, and air and water pollution. The program drew upon trends in human behavior going back to the year 1900. The Club of Rome hoped that World One would point out any problems humanity would need to solve along the way.

But when Forrester fed the data into World One, the program produced an unexpected result. It predicted the end of civilization—total global collapse—by the year 2040.

Over the decades since World One was created, MIT scientists have continued to update the program with new global data. But it continues to predict the end of civilization by around 2040.

Now, before you panic, I need to point out that the Club of Rome, which funded the World One project, is a pessimistic organization cofounded by financier David Rockefeller and other globalists. The Club of Rome has been predicting doom and gloom ever since its founding in 1968. I suspect that World One predicts the kind of future it is paid to predict. I don't think you should circle the year 2040 on your calendar as the year of doomsday.

The only predictions I have any confidence in are found in the Word of God—including what Paul writes in 2 Timothy 3. He tells us that in the last days all human society will become coarse and brutish. As you read Paul's words, think about the people all around you today.

> But mark this: There will be terrible times in the last days. People will be lovers of themselves, lovers of money, boastful, proud, abusive, disobedient to their parents, ungrateful, unholy, without love, unforgiving, slanderous, without self-control, brutal, not lovers of the good,

treacherous, rash, conceited, lovers of pleasure
rather than lovers of God—having a form of
godliness but denying its power. Have nothing
to do with such people.

—2 Timothy 3:1–5

At the beginning of chapter 3, the apostle Paul
takes a sharp turn. That is why Paul begins this section with a conjunction—the word *but*. He writes:
"*But* mark this..." This indicates a change in direction in his argument, a transition from Timothy's current situation to a future prophecy. Paul told Timothy,
"But mark *this*," meaning, "Timothy, realize *this*.
Understand *this*. Do not be surprised about *this*."

In the first two chapters of 2 Timothy, Paul has
been dealing with Timothy's experiences as a leader in
the first-century church. Beginning in chapter 3, Paul
reveals a prophecy about the days immediately prior to
the return of Jesus Christ.

Paul says, "There will be terrible times in the last
days." In Scripture, "the last days" speak of the time
between the first coming of Jesus and His second
coming. We are two thousand years away from His
first coming—which means, of course, we are much
closer to His second. Exactly how close, we don't know.

In these verses, Paul describes conditions that have
existed since the first century. For more than two
thousand years, people have been lovers of themselves,
lovers of money, boastful, proud, abusive, and on and
on. But as we come closer and closer to the return of

the Lord Jesus Christ, we will see these cruel human traits increase in intensity.

TIME TO RISE UP!

Jesus Himself said, "Nation will rise against nation, and kingdom against kingdom. There will be famines and earthquakes in various places. All these are the beginning of birth pains" (Matt. 24:7–8). We have always had wars, famines, and earthquakes, so why does Jesus refer to these signs as "the beginning of birth pains"? It's because these events will increase in frequency during the last days.

Jesus said it will be like a woman in labor. As the labor pains intensify and become more frequent and closer together, we know she is about to give birth. In the same way, we can know that as wars, famines, and earthquakes grow more intense and frequent, and as human beings become more self-centered, boastful, and violent, we can be sure the return of Jesus is imminent.

Today, in the twenty-first century, we see that evil is intensifying. In fact, evil is being accepted and glorified while the Christian faith and Christian morality are vilified as evil. The world is in turmoil as never before. Russia and China are more aggressive than ever before. Islam is more militant than ever. Threats against the nation of Israel are increasing. Groups that espouse godless communism are on the rise across Europe and America and into South America. Racial strife, which once seemed to be on the wane, has erupted into rioting and looting in American streets.

More and more churches are rejecting God's truth and siding with human rebellion. The Lord Jesus said in Matthew 16:18, "on this rock"—the rock of Peter's profession of faith in Jesus the Messiah—"I will build my church, and the gates of Hades will not overcome it." Jesus never said His people would be free from spiritual danger and harm, but He promised that the forces of sin would never overcome His church.

In Matthew 7:15, Jesus said, "Watch out for false prophets. They come to you in sheep's clothing, but inwardly they are ferocious wolves." And we have seen many false prophets arise in our time, seeking to deceive Christians and lead them into error.

As the days grow darker and hearts grow colder, the world becomes more dangerous and uncertain. Christians need to band together as a tightly knit community of faith. We need to uphold, encourage, and strengthen one another against the coming days.

When we see signs of civilization breaking down, hatred and violence on the rise, nations warring against nations, we mustn't let go of our faith in God. We mustn't let our hearts melt within us. Instead, we must stand firm and stand together as believers.

When Paul says, "There will be terrible times in the last days," he is using language that suggests the feeling of being surrounded by wild beasts or a raging sea. He is conveying the idea of a perilous and uncontrollable situation. We need to understand that no matter how terrible these times may be, God is on the throne and always will be on His throne. God will always be for His people. God will always be ready to give us the victory.

This is not a time for fear and doubt. This is a time to rise up and be the army of the living God.

In 2 Timothy 3:2–9, Paul gives us a portrait of the people who will trouble believers in the last days. Clearly, the people Paul describes are already multiplying in our society. They are here. They are among us. They are exactly as Paul portrays them.

In Paul's description, we can see the following three aspects of the people who will persecute the church in the last days:

1. Their moral conduct

2. Their religious zeal

3. Their militant fanaticism

1. THEIR MORAL CONDUCT

First let's look at their moral conduct. In three short verses, Paul gives us nineteen expressions by which he describes the wickedness of the persecutors of the church in the last days. The first and the last descriptions summarize their essential nature—they are "lovers of themselves" and are *not* "lovers of God" (vv. 2, 4).

In fact, five out of the nineteen descriptions have to do with love: "lovers of themselves," "lovers of money," "without love," "not lovers of the good," and "lovers of pleasure rather than lovers of God." We hear the word *love* used all the time in our world today. In fact, there is probably no more overused and misused word in the English language than love.

When people use the word *love* today, they usually refer to an emotion they feel, a sexual experience they selfishly indulge in, or some indefinable feeling they are searching for but can't put into words. These are all misdirected, misguided notions of love, and they are no more genuine than the love Paul speaks of—love of self, love of money, or love of pleasure.

The world does not understand the love God has shown to us in Jesus Christ—a love that the Greek New Testament calls *agape*. It's the kind of love Paul has defined so thoroughly and precisely:

> Love is patient, love is kind. It does not envy, it does not boast, it is not proud. It does not dishonor others, it is not self-seeking, it is not easily angered, it keeps no record of wrongs. Love does not delight in evil but rejoices with the truth. It always protects, always trusts, always hopes, always perseveres. Love never fails.
>
> —1 Corinthians 13:4–8

The world will continue talking about false and misguided ideas of love even as our civilization sinks into hatred, violence, and brutality. Relationships will break down. Society will rip apart at the seams. People will become proud, arrogant, and abusive—and still they will talk about love without any idea of what the word truly means.

Paul also says that in the last days people will be "boastful, proud, abusive, disobedient to their parents, ungrateful" (2 Tim. 3:2). We see these destructive behaviors in many homes today. These attitudes and behaviors are rampant among young people and have been so since the beginning of history. It's common for adolescents to think they are the center of the universe, they know more than their parents, and they are entitled to money, a car, a smartphone, and total freedom without any responsibility. It's common for adolescents to be ungrateful for all their parents have sacrificed and provided for them.

Some young people demonstrate bitter resentment toward their parents. And let's be honest, no one has ever had perfect parents. I did not have perfect parents, and I have certainly not been a perfect parent. But young people still owe a debt of respect, obedience, and gratitude to their parents.

If you are a young person and you feel inclined to rebel against your parents and disobey them, please understand this: you do not have to agree with your parents, but you must obey and respect your parents. As Paul wrote, "Children, obey your parents in the Lord, for this is right" (Eph. 6:1). Your parents may not always be right, but obedience is always right. Of course, there are a few exceptions to this rule. For example, if you have a parent who is abusive and who tries to make you sin against God, then you must obey God, not the abusive parent.

The far more common problem in families today is children who feel entitled to be continually entertained and who think they know more than their parents. One of the most overused expressions among young people today is, "I'm bored!" What they are really saying is, "I want more screen time" or "I want more video game time." As parents, we need to offer creative solutions to the complaint of "I'm bored." For example, we could cure that boredom by providing chores and suggesting wholesome activities such as straightening their rooms, weeding the flower bed, planting a garden, or volunteering at either a retirement home or tutoring program.

I have always found that the most pleasant, humble, kind, and grateful young people are those who are too busy doing good works to complain about boredom. They are investing their spare time serving others. Young people who never do chores, never serve others, and have everything handed to them on a silver platter almost always grow up spoiled and ungrateful. But young people who learn the value of work and the value of helping others develop a habit of gratitude toward God and their parents.

Paul said one of the signs that you are living in the last days is when you see children who lack humility, respect, affection, and gratitude toward their parents. These positive qualities tend to characterize children raised in Christian homes. Of course, some children raised in loving Christian families still manage to go astray (frequently because of bad influences from their peers).

We must reach out to children who have never been taught about the love of Jesus. We need to invite them to Sunday school, vacation Bible school, Child Evangelism's Good News Clubs, and other outreach events for kids. As Christian parents, we need to get involved in hosting Boy Scout and Girl Scout troops, coaching youth sports, tutoring kids, and taking on other endeavors where we can influence kids who have no Christian role model in the home. We need to see our children's peers as a mission field, ripe for harvest.

If we are living in the last days, we must reach out to the children and grown-ups around us with the good news of Jesus Christ. We need to save as many as we can while there is still time.

DISREGARD FOR GODLINESS AND TRUTH

Paul then moves to more forms of ungodliness, describing people in the last days who are "unholy, without love, unforgiving, slanderous, without self-control, brutal, not lovers of the good, treacherous, rash, conceited, lovers of pleasure rather than lovers of God" (vv. 2–4).

He is describing people who are bitter and vengeful, who destroy reputations and spread scandal, who engage in sinful habits without self-control, who haven't a shred of moral decency or compassion, who care only about power and care nothing about the truth.

The people Paul describes dominate our news media. Cable news shows are frequently smearing reputations and spreading lies to achieve a partisan political goal. One leading *New York Times Magazine* editor declared in 2021, "All journalism is activism." In other words, journalists should not objectively report the facts, but should indoctrinate their readers in a certain point of view. Another former *New York Times* freelance editor wrote a piece titled "I'm a Biased Journalist and I'm Okay With That." A Stanford University journalism professor declared that the journalistic profession needs to "free itself from this notion of objectivity" and advocate instead for his version of "social justice."[2]

Journalists who believe activism is more important than objectivity are people who have an utter disregard for the truth. They are not engaged in journalism as we have always understood it. They are engaged in propaganda and deception. They care only about power. They will tell you that they are pursuing social justice, but as we have already seen, the only way to achieve justice and change society for the better is through the gospel of Jesus Christ.

2. THEIR RELIGIOUS ZEAL

Paul warned that in the last days there would be people "having a form of godliness but denying its power. Have nothing to do with such people" (2 Tim.

3:5). In other words, people will be very religious and very zealous, but they will serve a profane religion that denies the power of the one true God.

It may come as a shock to you that many of the people Paul warns against—the dangerous and ruthless enemies of the church who will arise in the last days—are *devoutly religious people.* Yet these warnings should not surprise us. Throughout the Bible, in both the Old and New Testaments, we find warning after warning against false religion.

For example, the Old Testament prophet Amos warned Israel during the reign of Jeroboam II that while there was a boom in religious activity, there was an utter collapse in genuine faith and morality. Wanton immorality had even invaded the religious practices of Israel at that time.

> They lie down beside every altar on garments taken in pledge. In the house of their god they drink wine taken as fines.
>
> —AMOS 2:8

The prophet Isaiah deplored the same religious hypocrisy in the southern kingdom of Judah:

> When you spread out your hands in prayer, I hide my eyes from you; even when you offer many prayers, I am not listening. Your hands are full of blood!
>
> —ISAIAH 1:15

I remember a day in 2011 when I was interviewed at the CNN television studio in Atlanta. During a commercial break, I leaned toward the anchorman and said, "Why don't you visit our church one Sunday?"

His eyes widened and he said, "No!"

I was taken aback by his strong reaction. I said, "Why won't you come?"

"Because," he said, "you'll tell me I'm going to hell. I go to a church that tells me there is no hell."

I was shocked by his answer. I had never met this man before the producer introduced us. I didn't think he knew who I was. He evidently knew that at The Church of The Apostles we preach the uncompromised Word of God.

This man was a churchgoer—but he didn't want the uncompromised truth. He wanted a religion that would flatter him and tell him what he wanted to hear. I don't know what church he attended, but I do know there are many churches like the one he described.

In Matthew 23:25, Jesus stood up to the false teachers known as Pharisees and said, "You clean the outside of the cup and dish, but inside they are full of greed and self-indulgence." Hypocritical religion has been around since the time of Amos and Isaiah, the time of Jesus and Paul, and it is still with us today. It will become more and more prevalent as we move into the last days.

People will be very religious, but their religion will be false and hypocritical. It will have an outward form of godliness, but those who practice it will deny God's power. We see forms of such religion already today. In so-called "progressive Christianity" or "the emerging church," they have a form of godliness. They read selected passages of Scripture, talk about Jesus, and selectively quote His words.

But they don't preach a gospel of salvation by grace through faith in Jesus Christ. They ignore those Scripture passages that speak of heaven, hell, eternal life, the resurrection, the miracles of Jesus, and the second coming. Or if they do speak of such things, they treat them as metaphors, not literal realities. They have an outward form of godliness, but they deny God's power. They have replaced the gospel of Jesus Christ with a social gospel. They have replaced faith and salvation with a secular political agenda.

Anytime religion becomes an outward show, going through the motions of the liturgy, dropping a few dollars in the collection plate, or using religious-sounding words to impress others, we come under the condemnation of this passage in 2 Timothy. We are guilty of having a form of godliness but denying its power. Our religion is an outward show without an inward reality. It is a religion without confession, repentance, and moral demands.

Religion without godly moral conduct is a dead religion. Religious zeal without Christ is misguided zeal.

Authentic faith combines both a genuine godliness and the power of God. Authentic faith combines spiritual worship and godly living. Authentic faith talks the talk and walks the walk. Authentic faith shows sinners the way home to healing, forgiveness, and eternal life.

3. THEIR MILITANT FANATICISM

Next, Paul warns that militant fanaticism will arise in the church in the last days. He writes:

> They are the kind who worm their way into homes and gain control over gullible women, who are loaded down with sins and are swayed by all kinds of evil desires, always learning but never able to come to a knowledge of the truth. Just as Jannes and Jambres opposed Moses, so also these teachers oppose the truth. They are men of depraved minds, who, as far as the faith is concerned, are rejected. But they will not get very far because, as in the case of those men, their folly will be clear to everyone.
>
> —2 TIMOTHY 3:6–9

Paul is preparing us to recognize these godless lovers of self who not only profess religion of a very superficial kind, but who also want to impose their godless, immoral religion on others. They are on a mission to conform every church to their militant fanaticism. They are hostile toward biblical morality. They will seek to intimidate anyone who disagrees with them.

They claim biblical morality is unloving. If you, as a Bible-believing Christian, refuse to accept and affirm people who are living an openly sinful lifestyle, they will accuse you of being judgmental, unloving, unfair, mean, rigid, narrow-minded, and even unchristian. And they will say it with a smug, self-satisfied smile. Yet behind the smile they are scheming to intimidate and silence Bible-believing Christians.

Paul tells us that such people take advantage of weak women (and, I dare say, weak men). For example, these people frequently devalue motherhood, diminish human life, and demean godly women who make godly choices. They refer to abortion as "reproductive justice." They manipulate emotions and deceive the unsuspecting. They use double-talk—speaking out of both sides of their mouths, saying one thing to one group and another thing to another group, but never being honest about their real intent to destroy biblical Christianity.

Paul compares the deception of these false and fanatical religious teachers to Jannes and Jambres, two of Pharaoh's magicians. They counterfeited the miracles of Moses by using magic tricks. The story is found in Exodus 7, but the magicians are not mentioned by name in the Book of Exodus. However, there was an ancient legendary book, *The Apocryphon of Jannes and Jambres*, that claimed to tell the story of those two magicians. Only fragments of that book still exist today, but Paul was undoubtedly familiar with it.

The apostle is telling us that false teachers in the church who oppose God's truth are like those Egyptian magicians who opposed Moses. Paul preached the gospel; Moses taught God's law. Both preached God's uncompromised truth. Therefore, those who reject the infallible Word of God and preach a different "gospel" are preaching "black magic." They are committing the horrible sin of Jannes and Jambres.

Paul wants you to know that you do not need to be intimidated by these religious fanatics and false teachers. They may sway the weak-minded and the weak in faith. Their kind of falsehood may become fashionable in society. It may even become a majority religion in our world, and its anti-biblical teachings may be used to persecute genuine Christians who stand firm on the Word of God. But stand firm!

Whatever the future may bring, don't surrender. Don't be intimidated. Don't compromise. Never give up on biblical truth.

THE PROBLEM IN
THE PULPITS

In 2019, the Barna research group released the results of a study titled "Pastors Face Communication Challenges in a Divided Culture." The study found that half of American pastors are afraid to preach biblical morality regarding such "hot-button issues" as "the LGBT community, same-sex marriage rights, abortion, sexual morality and politics." The study also found that pastors are not only afraid of being criticized by the world, but of being opposed by their own church members. Here's a statement from the Barna study:

We wanted to know if pastors felt limited or pressured when it comes to speaking about controversial topics. Half of Christian pastors say they frequently (11%) or occasionally (39%) feel limited in their ability to speak out on moral and social issues because people will take offense. The other half of pastors say they only rarely (30%) or never (20%) feel limited in this way. When asked to identify the source of the concerns, pastors are much more likely to say that they feel limited by those inside the church than those outside. In other words, the reactions of those in the pews are most on the minds of today's pastors.[3]

Soon after this study was released, I appeared with two other pastors on *Fox & Friends* on the Fox News Channel.

I said, "In the end, you have to decide, are you going to please God and obey his Word, or are you going to please people? Now, as Bible-believing Christians, we love everybody. We have no [phobias] because love casts out fear. [There is] no fear in Christ. Nonetheless, as we love people, we must always say as pastors, 'Thus says the Lord.'...If it's in the Book, I'm going to preach it.

"All of us as pastors, we have dealt with families who have children...all sorts of lifestyles. And I always say to them, 'You love them, and you love them, and then you love them some more, but you never compromise your conviction.' You say, 'I love you, but I don't approve of what you're doing.'

"It's speaking the truth in love and not [being] afraid because you are serving God and you're serving the congregation. And you're speaking for God to the congregation. The moment that is reversed, we're gonna please people and not gonna please God. We're in trouble. That's what's happening in America. The reason morality has gone out of the window is because… the preachers have ceased to preach the truth."[4]

Several years ago an ordained minister in a mainline denomination was named headmaster of a prominent Christian school. His first order of business after taking charge was to remove the school from its biblical foundation. He attracted many non-Christian students to the school, and this gave non-Christian parents leverage over what was being taught.

Even after this man took charge, vestiges of biblical Christianity remained in the curricula and in the daily classroom prayers. As a result, non-Christian parents contacted the headmaster and complained about the classroom prayers because the prayers were offered in the name of Jesus.

So, in an effort to appease the non-Christian parents, the headmaster sent a letter out to all the parents. He wrote, "When we end prayers with the words 'in Jesus' name,' we affirm Jesus' dependence on our prayers."

A Christian parent showed me that letter, and I could not believe my eyes. *Jesus* depends on *our* prayers? *Jesus* is dependent on *us*?

I contacted the headmaster, and I read that statement to him and asked, "Did you really mean to say that? This is heresy! This is falsehood! No! A million times, no! We approach the Father in the name of Jesus because Jesus Himself said, 'No one comes to the Father except through me' (John 14:6) and 'My Father will give you whatever you ask in my name' (John 16:23). We pray in the name of Jesus because He is the image of the invisible God—God incarnate. He does not depend on our prayers. We experience power when *we depend on* Him in prayer."

I didn't change this man's mind. Frankly, he wasn't interested in what the Bible had to say about prayer. He is the kind of false teacher Paul warned us about.

EVIL SEEDS AND GOOD SEEDS

Paul concludes this section of his letter with good news about the fanatical false teachers that have infiltrated the church: "But they will not get very far because, as in the case of those men, their folly will be clear to everyone" (2 Tim. 3:9).

In Matthew, Jesus told a parable about the times in which we live and about the last days. He said:

> The kingdom of heaven is like a man who sowed good seed in his field. But while everyone was sleeping, his enemy came and sowed weeds among the wheat, and went away. When the

wheat sprouted and formed heads, then the weeds also appeared....

The servants asked him, "Do you want us to go and pull them up?"

"No," he answered, "because while you are pulling the weeds, you may uproot the wheat with them. Let both grow together until the harvest. At that time I will tell the harvesters: First collect the weeds and tie them in bundles to be burned; then gather the wheat and bring it into my barn."

—MATTHEW 13:24–26, 28–30

Here is the key to the parable: The field is the world, and the owner of the field is God. The good seed is the gospel. The stalks of wheat are genuine Christians. The enemy, of course, is Satan, and the weeds are false Christians.

God has sown the seed of the gospel throughout the world. Many true believers have sprouted up and taken root. But Satan has also sown seed in the world—and the weeds known as false believers have sprung up right alongside the true believers. We have seen the weeds and wheat growing together ever since the church was founded. But today, in the twenty-first century, we see this phenomenon taking place as never before.

Satan has sown his evil seeds in the very heart of many evangelical churches. Paul is saying, "Do not be discouraged. Do not be intimidated. Do not let the weeds choke out your wheat. Above all, do not allow yourself to become infected by the weeds among you."

Stand bold and firm. Don't give up hope and don't give up the gospel. Soon—very soon—you and I will be caught up in the air to meet our beloved Lord and Savior. Soon—very soon—you and I will hear the shout of the archangel and the sound of the trumpet. Soon—very soon—you and I will see Jesus face to face, and we shall reign with Him in heaven. Soon—very soon—He will wipe away all our tears, and we will be with Him forever and ever.

Will you be there?

CHAPTER 6

THE PRESSURE TO CONFORM

Solomon Asch (1907–1996) was a Polish-American psychologist. In the early 1950s, he developed an experiment that has become a classic guide to understanding human behavior, the Asch Conformity Experiment. He first conducted the experiment at Swarthmore College. He invited fifty male students to take a "vision test."

In the "vision test" in groups of eight, seven of the students were told in advance the answer they should give to each question. The eighth person, the actual test subject, was led to believe the other seven students were real participants like himself. Then Asch would show all the participants two cards like these:[1]

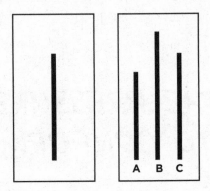

Each person had to say out loud which compar-ison line (A, B, or C) was most like the line in the first picture. Clearly, the matching line is C. But as prearranged, the first seven participants would some-times give the same wrong answer. In some tests, all seven would say A. In other tests, all seven would say B. The last person in line—the actual test subject—would hear the other seven participants give the wrong answer. Each participant took the "vision test" mul-tiple times. Though it was obvious that the majority was wrong, about 75 percent of participants conformed to the majority at least one time. Only 25 percent stood their ground and refused to conform.

Most of those who conformed later admitted they knew their answers were wrong, but they went along with the majority out of fear of being criticized. But a few said the majority made them doubt their own per-ception. They thought, "If everyone else is choosing A or B, then I must be mistaken to think it's C."

This experiment shows that peer pressure can

make people change their behavior to conform to the majority. It can even make people doubt what they know to be true.[2]

CONFORMING TO THE WORLD OR TO CHRIST

The pressure to conform is not limited to the young. It's universal among people of all ages. And the undeniable fact is we will either be conformed to the image of Christ or we will conform to the world. There is no middle ground. So if we want the church to stand firm for biblical truth, we must train and disciple Christians—especially young Christians—in how to be conformed to the image of Christ.

Again and again, the Bible speaks of being conformed to the image of Christ:

> For those God foreknew he also predestined to be conformed to the image of his Son, that he might be the firstborn among many brothers and sisters.
>
> —ROMANS 8:29

> And just as we have borne the image of the earthly man, so shall we bear the image of the heavenly man [Jesus].
>
> —1 CORINTHIANS 15:49

> ...until we all reach unity in the faith and in the knowledge of the Son of God and become

> mature, attaining to the whole measure of the
> fullness of Christ.
>
> —Ephesians 4:13

As we grow more and more conformed to the image of Christ in our character, our prayer life, and the boldness of our witness, we become increasingly less susceptible to the pressure of the world. When the image of Christ becomes indelibly stamped on our personality, the world simply cannot squeeze us into its mold.

But if we are not building Christlikeness into our character every day, the surrounding culture will shape us into its image. Our thinking, our behavior, and our perceptions will all be molded by the world. We will have conformed to the world, and the image of Christ within us will be *deformed.*

Some of the most influential people in our godless world are celebrities. Some people are famous because of their accomplishments while other people are famous merely for being famous. There are some celebrities who never appear on TV, in the movies, or in the news, but are famous for developing a following on the internet.

There is no entrance exam a person must pass to become a celebrity. Doctors must be certified and licensed to practice medicine. Lawyers must pass the bar exam to practice law. But celebrities don't even have to pass a drug or breathalyzer test (and many couldn't), yet they have become role models and influencers in our society.

That's why the apostle Paul warns us against patterning ourselves after the wrong role model.

"BUT AS FOR YOU. . ."

In the second half of 2 Timothy 3, Paul urges us to begin preparing now to stand our ground in the last days. He writes:

> You, however, know all about my teaching, my way of life, my purpose, faith, patience, love, endurance, persecutions, sufferings—what kinds of things happened to me in Antioch, Iconium and Lystra, the persecutions I endured. Yet the Lord rescued me from all of them. In fact, everyone who wants to live a godly life in Christ Jesus will be persecuted, while evildoers and impostors will go from bad to worse, deceiving and being deceived. But as for you, continue in what you have learned and have become convinced of, because you know those from whom you learned it, and how from infancy you have known the Holy Scriptures, which are able to make you wise for salvation through faith in Christ Jesus. All Scripture is God-breathed and is useful for teaching, rebuking, correcting and training in righteousness, so that the servant of God may be thoroughly equipped for every good work.
>
> —2 Timothy 3:10–17

Paul begins with the words, "You, however." That word *however* is a conjunction that indicates a contrast. In this section, Paul draws a contrast between the ungodly character of false preachers, as we saw in the last chapter, and the godly character of a true minister of the gospel. And the role model Paul focuses on—himself.

"You, however, know all about my teaching," he writes, "my way of life, my purpose, faith, patience, love, endurance, persecutions, sufferings—what kinds of things happened to me in Antioch, Iconium and Lystra, the persecutions I endured." Timothy, who was much like you and me, was tempted to show weakness and timidity in pressure situations. Timothy was well aware of the struggles and sufferings Paul had endured—so Paul offered himself as a role model for Timothy and for us.

Paul wrote this letter precisely because he knew Timothy's weak points. He was deeply concerned because he knew the day of his departure for heaven was approaching, and he would no longer be around to encourage Timothy in person. He wanted to leave this letter of encouragement so Timothy and future generations could read it for inspiration.

We saw in verse 10 a conjunction to indicate contrast, "You, however..." In verses 13 and 14, Paul again uses a conjunction for contrast, writing, "evildoers and impostors will go from bad to worse, deceiving and being deceived. *But as for you*, continue in what you have learned" (emphasis added).

Paul is drawing a sharp contrast. On one hand are the evildoers who deceive others and are themselves deceived. And on the other hand ("But as for you...") is Timothy, the servant of God and minister of the gospel. And Paul's message to Timothy is: Don't yield to worldly pressure. Don't succumb to worldly temptation. Don't let the world squeeze you into its mold.

ONLY ONE CUSTOMER

Conform to Christ or conform to the world. This is a consistent theme of the apostle Paul. Why does he hammer this theme was such intensity? It's because Paul knows how easily we fall into temptation. He knows how quickly we yield to pressure and criticism. He knows how prone we are to take the easy way out.

In Romans 12:2 Paul wrote, "Do not conform to the pattern of this world, but be transformed by the renewing of your mind. Then you will be able to test and approve what God's will is—his good, pleasing and perfect will."

Friend in Christ, if you are living for Jesus, sharing the good news with your friends and coworkers, taking a stand for biblical morality, operating your business according to godly principles, and proclaiming the good news on social media, you are coming under pressure. People are calling you names. They are telling you that your morality is rigid, narrow-minded, or unloving.

Why is this happening? It's because we live in a

post-Christian age. We live in an age hostile to Jesus and His gospel.

Instead of advancing into the world and taking territory for Jesus Christ, the world is infiltrating the church. The minds of many in the church today are drenched with the ideas and ideologies of our worldly culture. We have been slow to realize the church is gradually conforming itself to the world.

I recently heard of a pastor of a megachurch who announced to his congregation, "Don't call me 'Pastor' anymore. This church is a corporation, and I am the CEO."

Now, there's nothing wrong with being a corporate CEO. I love CEOs. Some of my best friends are CEOs. In fact, titles really do not mean a great deal to me. But why would the pastor of a church not want to be called "Pastor"? Why would he prefer a worldly title such as "CEO"? Why would he be ashamed of being called "a co-laborer with Christ" or an "undershepherd of the church"?

I have deep respect for godly businessmen and businesswomen. Many are leaders and pillars of our church. But a business is fundamentally different from a church. The purpose of a business is to make a profit while serving the community. The purpose of the church is to preach the gospel, advance the kingdom, equip the saints for ministry, and minister to the poor and needy. A business, in order to stay in business, is focused on pleasing its customers. A church is focused on pleasing the Lord Jesus Christ and Him alone.

If you ask the pastor, "Who is your customer?" and the pastor answers, "The people in my congregation," *that's the wrong answer!* Any pastor who gives that answer is in the wrong line of work. The only right answer is, "I have only one customer, and His name is Jesus of Nazareth."

Jesus is the Lord of the church. He is the One we must obey to the uttermost. He is the One we must please to the uttermost.

Any pastor who has a goal of pleasing people in the congregation is doomed to failure. That is an unrealistic, unreachable goal. You can never satisfy the congregation because the congregation is made up of different kinds of people from different backgrounds with a variety of expectations. Anything you do that pleases one group of people will displease another group. You can't please all the people all the time.

DON'T LOOK FOR "McCHURCH"

So what's a Christian to do? Set your sights on pleasing Jesus alone. If He is pleased, nothing else matters. Most important of all, if you seek to please the Lord Jesus with all your heart, soul, and mind, everyone around you will be blessed.

Are you searching for the perfect church that will meet all your needs? Perhaps you have gone from one church to the next, thinking, "This church has good music, but I didn't care for the sermon. That church has a good Sunday school for the kids, but we had to park too far away." And on and on, weighing pros against cons, in search of the "perfect church."

I can absolutely guarantee that the perfect church does not exist. There is no church on the face of the earth that can meet *all* your needs.

The true church of Jesus Christ is not a "McChurch" where you can order the gospel tailored to your needs as if it were a burger and fries to go. The true church of Jesus Christ does not exist to make you happy. Yet the message you hear in many churches today is, "God wants to make you happy!"

Jesus did not build His church to meet your needs. The purpose of the church, the purpose of the pastors and teachers, and the purpose of the Bible study leaders, the elders, and the deacons is not to take you by the hand and meet all your needs. The purpose of the church is to place your hand in the strong hand of Jesus.

And Jesus alone will meet all your needs according to His riches in glory (Phil. 4:19).

Paul's message to Timothy is not, "Be all things to all people. Make sure you keep your customers satisfied. Focus on pleasing everybody and meeting everybody's needs." No, his message to Timothy is, "Stand firm in what you have learned from me. Stand firm in doctrinal purity. Stand firm in following God's purpose in your life. Stand firm in the face of pressure and persecution."

HOW TO ESCAPE PERSECUTION

In 2 Timothy 3:12, Paul states a key principle of the Christian life we should never forget. He writes, "In fact, everyone who wants to live a godly life in Christ Jesus will be persecuted." Do you see any exceptions in that statement? I don't. Paul is saying that a person living a godly life will *always, always, always* arouse antagonism among the ungodly.

If you are a committed and godly Christian living in a non-Christian home, you *will* face ridicule and persecution. If you are a Christian living out your faith in a secular workplace, you will experience some form of opposition from your coworkers and employer. You may even be denied promotions or raises.

A godly Christian may even suffer persecution from the institutional church and fellow church members. If you challenge apostasy or abusive behavior in your church, you will likely find that many (including church leaders) will turn against you, attack you, and defend the apostates and abusers.

All those who would live a godly life in Christ Jesus will be persecuted. This was true when Jesus walked the earth, and it is still true today. Jesus Himself said, "If the world hates you, keep in mind that it hated me first. If you belonged to the world, it would love you as its own. As it is, you do not belong to the world, but I have chosen you out of the world. That is why the world hates you" (John 15:18–19).

There are two kinds of people in this world who will never suffer persecution. First, there are the Christians who cloister themselves in a monastery on a mountaintop and never come in conflict with this sinful, hostile world. They have escaped the pressures of the world by withdrawing from it. Second, there are those who do not walk with Christ but are conformed to the world. They will never face persecution because they are not distinct from the world in any way. They have escaped the pressures of this world by surrendering and conforming. Some of these people call themselves Christians, but they have abandoned the biblical definition of a follower of Christ. They have replaced the gospel of Jesus Christ with worldly ideologies.

Whether they call themselves Christians or not, these are the people Paul describes in 2 Timothy 3:13: "Evildoers and impostors will go from bad to worse, deceiving and being deceived."

If you want to escape persecution, these are your options: withdraw from the world or conform to the world. You cannot live a godly life, engaged in spiritual warfare, and escape persecution. If you serve Jesus Christ, persecution is your lot.

Paul does not want Timothy or us to join a monastery. And he certainly doesn't want us to conform to the world. His next statement to Timothy is, "But as for you, continue in what you have learned and have become convinced of, because you know those from whom you learned it" (v. 14).

But as for you, faithful Christian who seeks to

uphold godly living, who stands firm on biblical truth, and who never gives up, no matter the cost, continue in what you have learned. Continue to cling tightly to the Word of truth.

WILLING TO PAY THE PRICE

A friend of mine is a businessman who does billions of dollars of trade in Africa. He was once offered a business deal worth hundreds of millions of dollars, but the deal was dishonest and unethical, so he walked away from it. He paid a hefty price to maintain his Christian character.

A year or so later, he made a billion-dollar deal, and it was completely honest and ethical. Perhaps that was God's reward for making the right decision on the earlier deal. But even if that bigger deal hadn't come along, he made the right decision. He followed Jesus. He obeyed the Scriptures. He kept his conscience clean. And that is worth more than all the money in the world.

Following Jesus can cost you dearly. It can cost you friendships. It can cause you to be ridiculed and persecuted. It can even cost you a career or millions of dollars. Even if it costs you everything you have, keep following Jesus.

Young man, it doesn't matter if the young lady you are dating has the face of an angel—if she is pressuring you to commit sin, walk away.

Young lady, it doesn't matter if the young man you

are dating looks like he just stepped off the cover of a romance novel—if he is pressuring you to commit sin, walk away.

Whatever it costs you to follow Jesus, be willing to pay that price. Be willing to suffer persecution. Be willing to suffer loss. Be willing to suffer mockery. Jesus knows how you feel, and one day He will honor you and reward your faithfulness.

"But as for you, continue…" Stand firm. Persevere. Endure, even in times of oppression and opposition.

When persecution comes, the godly keep moving forward, upward, always advancing. The godly are eternally invincible.

The ungodly are on the road to destruction. They are intellectually and spiritually ruined. They go from bad to worse. Avoid false teachers. Reject their lies. Refute their deception.

Stand firm for the truth.

THE GREATEST LEGACY

The 1970s saw the birth of a movement known as the Church Growth Movement. Initially, the movement had good intentions, including a desire to fulfill the Great Commission and expand the church around the world. The movement, which took hold in several major seminaries and churches, sought to merge biblical principles with secular-based research and analysis of social trends. Over time, many in the Church Growth Movement became obsessed with growing the size of churches and building ministries that had the look of success.

Many churches built on church-growth strategies began to abandon such biblical subjects as sin, judgment, and hell. These churches were filling the pews and expanding their budgets, but they weren't making disciples. They weren't preaching the uncompromised Word of God. They were growing the institutional church, but they did so at the expense of advancing the *true* church of Jesus Christ.

Over the decades, waves of church-growth theologians and strategists came and went. They urged pastors to avoid certain stories in the Old Testament, the "hard sayings" of Jesus, and many of the "difficult teachings" of the apostle Paul. Many preachers took their advice. They have built large megachurches where people can hear a positive, feel-good message, but the gospel of Jesus Christ is never preached. These churches are rich in donations but spiritually bankrupt.

If these false teachers are right and there really is no sin, no coming judgment, no hell, and no need for forgiveness, then tell me why did Jesus come from heaven, die on the cross, and rise from the dead?

The apostle Paul knew false teachers would arise in the church and cast doubt upon the Word of God. They perform the same role Satan performed in the Garden of Eden, subtly asking, "Did God *really* say...?" (See Genesis 3:1.)

Paul affirms the truthfulness of the *entire* Word of God. He affirms the integrity of *all* of Scripture.

He declares the verbal inspiration of the *entire* Bible. Under the inspiration of the Holy Spirit, Paul declares that all of Scripture is "God-breathed."

He writes in 2 Timothy 3:15–16, "From infancy you have known the Holy Scriptures, which are able to make you wise for salvation through faith in Christ Jesus. All Scripture is God-breathed and is useful for teaching, rebuking, correcting and training in righteousness." The very Scriptures Timothy's mother and grandmother taught him had opened his heart to receive Jesus as Messiah, Lord, and Savior and prepared him to be a minister of the gospel.

Christian parent, I encourage you with every ounce of my being—*prepare your children to stand confidently upon the Word of God.* Prepare them to face spiritual battles to come. Teach them the good news of salvation by grace through faith in Jesus Christ.

The greatest legacy we can leave for our children and grandchildren is not a trust fund, a college fund, or a wall safe full of US savings bonds. The greatest and most enduring legacy we can leave our children and grandchildren is to immerse their minds, hearts, and souls in the beauty of God's Word.

The only antidote for deception is God's truth. So teach them a reverence for God's Word. Memorize scripture and teach your children to memorize scripture. Let your children see you applying the wisdom of God's Word to everyday life. Let them see you wrestle with difficult decisions by consulting the Word of God. Let them hear you reciting comforting passages from the Psalms or the Gospels in times of family crisis or loss.

When they see you reading the Bible, living the Bible, and applying the Bible to every life circumstance, they will grow to trust the Word of God.

REVEALING THE HEART OF GOD

Paul carefully underscores the reason we can trust the authority of God's Word. He tells us the Bible is inspired—that is, *God-breathed*. Some false teachers claim this means the Bible is "inspiring" to read. They say, as we read it, we feel "inspired" as if we are reading beautiful inspirational poetry.

In 2021, a "progressive" pastor in Tennessee posted a message to the church's Facebook page, stating:

> As Progressive Christians, we're open to the tensions and inconsistencies in the Bible. We know that it can't live up to impossible, modern standards. We strive to more clearly articulate what Scripture is and isn't.
>
> The Bible isn't:
> ✗ the Word of God
> ✗ self-interpreting
> ✗ a science book
> ✗ an answer/rule book
> ✗ inerrant or infallible
>
> The Bible is:

- a product of community
- a library of texts
- multi-vocal
- a human response to God
- living and dynamic[3]

This church's Facebook post was very popular and drew many comments from people who supported this demeaned and condescending view of the Bible. For example, one comment stated, "Wow, I'd never heard a church say that the Bible isn't the Word of God... and honestly that is so refreshing."[4]

What does it mean that the Bible "can't live up to impossible, modern standards"? It means our godless culture has judged the Bible and found it wanting. The Bible is not politically correct. The Bible is not in step with the progressive dogmas of the twenty-first century. The Bible isn't "woke."

I fear for those "progressive Christians" who have denied the truth Paul expressed in 2 Timothy 3:16. The Bible was brought into existence by the breath of the Holy Spirit. The Spirit moved through the minds of the writers of the Bible. God is the author, and they were the writers God had prepared for this task even before they were born. As God told Jeremiah, "Before I formed you in the womb I knew you, before you were born I set you apart; I appointed you as a prophet to the nations" (Jer. 1:5).

Each writer of the Bible had his own distinct style and vocabulary. Each book grew out of a special set of circumstances. Through it all, the Holy Spirit was breathing, inspiring, and guiding. The Bible writers were like sailors on a sailboat. They would hoist their sails, they would tack and move the tiller, but the breath of the Holy Spirit filled their sails and carried them wherever He willed. As the apostle Peter explained, "For prophecy never had its origin in the human will, but prophets, though human, spoke from God as they were carried along by the Holy Spirit" (2 Pet. 1:21).

The Old and New Testaments reveal to us the mind, heart, and character of God. If the Bible is not the Word of God, if it is merely a "library of texts" and a "human response to God," how can we learn anything about God from the Bible? Anyone who views the Bible from this so-called "progressive" perspective has no reason to know, believe, or trust anything about God. In fact, this "progressive" view has concluded that human beings have the right and the wisdom to judge the Bible. This is breathtaking arrogance.

Paul tells us that because the Bible is God-breathed, it is profitable for our instruction regarding salvation. It is "useful for teaching, rebuking, correcting and training in righteousness" (2 Tim. 3:16).

There is a principle implied in Paul's statement that we should not miss. Notice he does not say the Bible's primary purpose is to teach us about science, history, or the nature of the stars and galaxies. The Bible's primary purpose is to tell us how to be saved. Once we have been saved, the Scriptures open our eyes to understand that God created everything from nothing. He created human beings from dust, and He controls the galaxies, stars, and planets. God calculated the orbits of the heavenly bodies before they came into existence.

But the Bible's central theme, from Genesis to Revelation, is about how we can know God and be saved. The Bible is salvation's handbook. It tells us that salvation is only possible by grace through faith in Jesus Christ. The Old Testament foretold His coming. The Gospels told us, "Here He is! This is what He did in the days of His ministry. This is what He accomplished through the cross and the empty tomb." The rest of the New Testament tells us how to live in light of the salvation He brought us.

That's why those who would undermine biblical morality began by undermining the authority of God's Word. They say we must downplay certain parts of the Old Testament that are hard for progressive preachers to explain because these biblical texts deal with sin and judgment. Progressive Christians are embarrassed by the God of the Old Testament.

Down through the centuries, many have tried to demean, deconstruct, and marginalize God's Word. They thought their human wisdom was superior to the wisdom of the Bible. They thought this philosophical idea or that scientific notion rendered the Bible obsolete. But all who attack God's Word are doomed to fail.

Jesus is on the throne. The Word of God endures.

HOW GREAT IS OUR LOVE
FOR GOD'S WORD?

Are you broken? God's Word will mend your broken heart. Are you lonely? God's Word will comfort you. Are you burdened with guilt? God's Word will set you free. Are you full of bitterness and resentment? God's Word will show you how to forgive. Are you defeated and hopeless? God's Word will give you victory. Are you discouraged? God's Word will lift your spirit. Are you despondent? God's Word will give you peace that passes understanding. Are you lost? God's Word will light your pathway back to Him. As the psalmist wrote, "Your word is a lamp for my feet, a light on my path" (Ps. 119:105).

At the close of the third century, the Roman Empire was ruled by a tetrarchy of four emperors—Diocletian, Maximian, Galerius, and Constantius. Diocletian harbored an intense hatred toward Christians. He persuaded his fellow emperors to issue a series of edicts that took away the legal rights of Christians and required them to perform pagan sacrifices to the Roman gods. This time of oppression became known as the Great Persecution—a time when thousands of Christians were tortured and killed for their faith, from Roman Britain to North Africa and Palestine.

Christians were required by Roman law to turn over their scrolls of Old Testament and New Testament Scripture. The Roman officials would seize the precious Word of God and cast it onto a bonfire.

In Thibiuca, a town near Carthage in North Africa, a man named Felix, the bishop of the town, refused to surrender his scrolls of Scripture or tell the authorities where he had hidden them. Magnilian, the magistrate of Thibiuca, sent soldiers to arrest Felix. When Felix stood before Magnilian, he declared, "It would be better that I be burnt than those books."

Magnilian sent Felix to the Roman proconsul at Carthage. The proconsul turned him over to the prefect of the praetorium, one of the highest commanders in the Roman Empire. When Felix refused to surrender the Scriptures, the prefect had Felix shackled and loaded down with heavy irons. Felix was imprisoned in a dungeon for nine days then taken aboard a ship bound for Italy. He lay in the hold of the ship for four days without food or water, with horses standing on either side of him.

When Felix arrived in Italy, he was surprised to find Christians lining the streets, cheering him because the word of his faithfulness had already spread across Italy. The prefect brought Felix to the town of Venosa in southern Italy and ordered that Felix be released from his shackles and irons. Then the prefect gave him one last chance to confess and reveal the location of the hidden scrolls.

Felix boldly confessed he possessed the forbidden scrolls of God's Word, but he would never give them up. The prefect turned to his soldiers and ordered them to prepare the prisoner for execution.

As Felix placed his head upon the block, he gave

thanks to God for His mercy and declared that, to the moment of His sacrifice, he had remained true to Jesus Christ and his truth. Those were his last words before a Roman sword sent Felix into the presence of his Lord and Savior.[5]

Today the Roman Empire is no more, but God's Word endures.

Can you and I say we love God's Word as much as Felix, the bishop of Thibiuca? Could we face our persecutors and say, "It would be better that I be burnt than those books"?

How great is our love for God's Word?

CHAPTER 7

FACING THE COMING JUDGMENT

Rob Bell founded Mars Hill Bible Church in Michigan in 1999 and was pastor of the church until 2012. It became one of the fastest-growing churches in the United States. In 2011, he published a controversial book, *Love Wins*. That same year, *Time* magazine named him one of the "100 Most Influential People in the World."

The essential theme of *Love Wins* is that the doctrine of hell prevents people from coming to Christ. Bell expressed it this way: "It's been clearly communicated to many that this belief [the doctrine of hell] is a central truth of the Christian faith and to reject it is, in essence, to reject Jesus. This is misguided and toxic and ultimately subverts the contagious spread of Jesus' message of love, peace, forgiveness, and joy that our world desperately needs to hear."[1]

Notice that Bell made no mention of Jesus' message of salvation.

Bell's reasoning might fool anyone who is ignorant of the Bible. But careful students of the Bible know Jesus spoke very clearly and frequently about hell. In Luke 16, Jesus told the story of Lazarus and the rich fool, with a vivid description of hell. In Matthew 5, Jesus warned that it's better to lose an eye or a hand that causes you to sin than to be cast into hell. As my friend Albert Mohler wrote in his review of *Love Wins*, "Rob Bell uses his incredible power of literary skill and communication to unravel the Bible's message and to cast doubt on its teachings."[2]

Rob Bell advocates a number of unbiblical views, such as the notion that people can choose to be saved after death—in direct opposition to the clear teaching of Hebrews 9:27, which warns that "people are destined to die once, and after that to face judgment."

After leaving Mars Hill Bible Church, Bell pursued a career as a freelance speaker, writer, and podcast host. He continues to peddle his best-selling, highly acclaimed heresy, but at least he is no longer preaching it as a church pastor.

I fear for the souls of those who have been taken in by his clever worldly reasoning and his subtle subversion of the truth. It was with good reason that *Time* magazine named him one of the "100 Most Influential People in the World." He has a personal charm that is very persuasive among the biblically uninformed. A sizable cult of personality has grown up around Rob Bell.

PERSONALITY CULTS
IN THE CHURCH

A personality cult is a group of people who share an excessive and unquestioning devotion to a leader. Personality cults abound in the church today. In the Christian world, personality cult leaders often become popular and influential by preaching a "gospel" that deviates from the Word of God. These leaders often talk about Jesus and the Bible, quoting selected passages of Scripture (usually twisting their meaning). They use religious jargon and slogans to deceive the unwise.

It's easy to understand why some people want to believe in a God who tolerates sin and allows a second chance at salvation after death. That kind of false Christianity makes no demands; requires no repentance, conversion, or sanctification; and permits an "anything-goes" amorality. This false Christianity also has no need of a cross, shed blood, or atonement for sin.

Any preacher with a smooth sales pitch, a glib manner, and a feel-good "gospel" is going to attract a lot of followers. Any preacher who claims the Bible can be twisted to justify abortion and same-sex marriage is going to be very popular. People are looking for easy answers. They are eager to hear that they can get to heaven without having to change their way of life.

Friend in Christ, please hear me! A genuine believer's loyalty should never be to a pastor, a priest, a pope, or a denomination. A believer's loyalty should always be to the Lord Jesus Christ and the inspired and infallible holy Scripture.

Jesus said, "Watch out that no one deceives you" (Matt. 24:4). The New Testament warns us again and again against deceivers. It amazes me that today's false teachers—many of whom quote and twist Scripture with ease—don't look at the Bible's warnings against deceivers and tremble with fear! Don't they know what awaits them in the day of judgment? And yet they continue to deceive the unwary with their false doctrines.

The Bible tells us again and again that Satan is the master of deception. The Greek word for "deception" is *plánē*, which literally means to wander astray from the right path, to roam this way and that without any sense of direction. It can refer to one person deceiving another person and causing that person to stray, or it can refer to self-deception, leading ourselves astray with our own sinful lusts and self-will.

Satan is subtle. He's a master psychologist. He subtly invites us to step off the path of truth an inch at a time. He doesn't say, "Go have an adulterous affair." He slyly suggests, "A little harmless flirting with a coworker wouldn't hurt, would it?" He doesn't say, "You should become a drug addict." He slyly suggests, "Why don't you try it once, just to see what it's like?" He doesn't say, "Go rob a bank." He slyly suggests, "You could cut a few ethical corners, make some extra money, and no one would ever find out. Don't you deserve a little more income?"

Inch by inch by inch, and before you know it, you

are trapped in an affair, an addiction, or a crime. You find yourself doing things you never thought you would do. You got there by straying from the biblical path an inch at a time.

GENTLY NUDGED
OFF THE PATH

When I lived in Lebanon, I saw shepherds guarding their sheep along narrow mountain paths. If the sheep ever wandered just a few steps off the path, they would have fallen off a cliff. But I never saw a sheep fall. Why? Because they always followed the shepherd and stayed on the path.

If you follow Jesus, the Good Shepherd, He will keep you on the path of life. But Satan uses false shepherds—personality cult leaders—to lure the unwary away from the path to their destruction.

Satan doesn't come to us and say, "Deny the Bible, deny Jesus, and declare your complete rejection of God and the Christian faith." No, he comes to us and says, "A God of love wouldn't judge anyone for expressing love to another person outside of marriage, would He? A God of love would never condemn someone to hell for rejecting Jesus, would He? The Bible was written for another time and culture, so why, in the twenty-first century, should anyone have to live by its ancient prejudices?"

Satan appeals to human lust, human pride, human intellectual arrogance, and any other human weakness he can get his hooks into. Then he will subtly and gradually move a person from belief to questioning to doubt to apostasy and ultimately to unbelief. He will work through the twisted reasoning of personality cult leaders to gently nudge you off the path.

If you do not wake up in time, the humanistic, hedonistic "gospel" of these false teachers will lead you to destruction. The apostle Paul was keenly aware of this subtle deception. He knew that we are all capable of being deceived. Even someone who is on fire for Jesus at one point in life can be deceived at another point. Even a church founded on the gospel of Jesus Christ can be infiltrated by deception.

IN SEASON AND
OUT OF SEASON

In light of the threat of false teachers in the church, Paul begins the final chapter of his final letter with these solemn words:

> In the presence of God and of Christ Jesus, who will judge the living and the dead, and in view of his appearing and his kingdom, I give you this charge: Preach the word; be prepared in season and out of season; correct, rebuke and encourage—with great patience and careful instruction. For the time will come when people will not put up with sound doctrine. Instead, to suit their own desires, they will gather around them a great number of teachers to say what

their itching ears want to hear. They will turn their ears away from the truth and turn aside to myths. But you, keep your head in all situations, endure hardship, do the work of an evangelist, discharge all the duties of your ministry.

—2 Timothy 4:1–5

Unfortunately, the New International Version translation of verse 1 is weaker than Paul's original Greek language. Paul isn't merely saying, "I give you this charge." The Berean Literal Bible reads, "I *earnestly* declare before God and Christ Jesus..." (emphasis added). The New American Standard Bible reads: "I *solemnly* exhort you in the presence of God and of Christ Jesus..." (emphasis added). The World English Bible reads, "I *command* you therefore before God and the Lord Jesus Christ..." (emphasis added).

Paul structured this command in the same way one would take an oath before testifying in a court of law. Yet Paul's charge to Timothy is even more solemn and binding because he makes this charge in the court of heaven, and his witnesses are the holy Trinity.

What does Paul command Timothy to do? He commands him to be faithful to the entire Word of God, the entire gospel of Jesus Christ. He commands Timothy to speak what God has spoken—no less and no more.

Paul's command to Timothy and to us is we must not take liberty with God's Word. We must not soften it and make it more palatable to the world. We must not try to massage, improve, or repackage it as if it were a product to be marketed. Our responsibility toward God's Word is simple: "Preach the word; be prepared in season and out of season; correct, rebuke and encourage—with great patience and careful instruction" (v. 2).

Paul anticipates a question on many minds today. "What if we preach the gospel and people don't like it? What if people are offended by the gospel?" Paul's answer: "For the time will come when people will not put up with sound doctrine" (v. 3). In other words, Paul *guarantees* some people won't want to hear biblical truth. They won't put up with sound doctrine. They'll reject it. They'll get angry. They'll persecute those who preach it.

The apostle's counsel to Timothy is, in effect, "If people don't like the gospel, that's not your problem. You just keep preaching the Word because you are preaching to please God, not people. You should only be concerned about God's opinion."

PROCLAIM THE TRUTH
WITH *URGENCY*

Paul commands Timothy to proclaim God's truth in three specific ways:

1. He must proclaim the Word of truth with *urgency.*

2. He must proclaim the Word of truth with *relevance*.

3. He must proclaim the Word of truth with *patience*, not expecting immediate results.

First, let's look at what it means to proclaim the truth with urgency. Paul wrote, "Be prepared in season and out of season....For the time will come when people will not put up with sound doctrine" (vv. 2–3). Be ready to share the gospel at any moment—in season, out of season, anytime of the day or night, whether it's convenient or inconvenient. Always be on call to share the good news with others. Be alert for opportunities to share the gospel. Never lose your sense of urgency.

Why must we proclaim the Word of truth with urgency? Because the stakes are so high. The eternal destination of the people around you depends on whether they hear the gospel. You may be the only Christian in someone's life. If they don't hear the good news from you, where will they hear it?

Suppose you walk outside and see your neighbor's house on fire. What would you do? You could say to yourself, "Well, I'm sure somebody will tell my neighbor he has a fire problem, but I better mind my own business." Or you could say, "I'm kind of busy right now. I have some errands to do. When I get back, I'll go tell my neighbor his house is on fire."

That's not how you would respond. A house fire

is a crisis, and you would respond with urgency. You would run to your neighbor's house, bang on his door, and say, "Get out now! Your house is on fire! It's a matter of life and death!"

Paul is telling Timothy and us that there is nothing more urgent than the gospel. People are dying and going into eternity without Jesus Christ. Their eternal destiny is on fire, and we must do all we can to save them. If we have even an ounce of human compassion, we have to knock on the door of their lives and plead with them to be saved.

This doesn't mean we badger people with the gospel. It means we are constantly alert to opportunities to share the good news of Jesus Christ. We must be ready to share the moment they give us an opening.

The phrase "in season and out of season" means that we must be ready at all times—including inconvenient times. We must be ready even if it means we lose sleep. We must be ready even if it means we are late for an appointment. We must be ready even if it costs us time and money.

Christians are always on duty and must always be ready to share the good news with a sense of urgency.

PROCLAIM THE TRUTH
WITH *RELEVANCE*

We must apply God's truth with *relevance*. We must bring God's truth to bear on the real-life circumstances of the people around us. We use God's Word to "correct, rebuke and encourage." Paul uses these three different words because they represent three different ways of applying God's Word to people's lives.

When we see people straying from the path of God's will, we use Scripture to *correct* them and lead them back to a righteous way of living. When we see people falling into sin or teaching false ideas, we use Scripture to *rebuke* them and confront their error. When we see people who are fearful and doubting, we use Scripture to *encourage* them and strengthen their faith.

This is exactly how Jesus used Scripture. He corrected, rebuked, and encouraged, using the power of God's Word to change minds and hearts. Here are just a few examples.

When Jesus was confronted by the Pharisees because His disciples didn't wash their hands before eating, He turned the tables on them, showing them how their traditions violated God's commands to "honor your father and your mother" (Exod. 20:12). That was Jesus *correcting*.

When Jesus was tempted by Satan in the wilderness, He responded to Satan's twisted lies with the truth of Scripture, quoting three passages from the Book of Deuteronomy. Jesus also rebuked the Sadducees, who taught that there was no resurrection of the dead, by quoting the words of God to Moses in Exodus 3:6. That was Jesus *rebuking*.

In the Sermon on the Mount in Matthew 5, Jesus cited passages from Exodus, Deuteronomy, and Leviticus that dealt with murder, adultery, divorce, and enemies. Then He encouraged the people to go deeper into righteousness by repenting of hate, lust, and making oaths. That was Jesus *encouraging*.

When we apply the Word of God to the real situations of people's lives, God is able to use His Word to touch people at their level. So our task is to make the Word relevant to their lives.

If you see someone who is troubled and anxious, share the words of Jesus to His fearful disciples, "Peace I leave with you; my peace I give you. I do not give to you as the world gives. Do not let your hearts be troubled and do not be afraid" (John 14:27).

If you have a friend who is suffering from exhaustion and burnout, share these words of the Lord Jesus, "Come to me, all you who are weary and burdened, and I will give you rest. Take my yoke upon you and learn from me, for I am gentle and humble in heart, and you will find rest for your souls. For my yoke is easy and my burden is light" (Matt. 11:28–30). Or this word of Old Testament encouragement, "He gives strength to the weary and increases the power of the weak" (Isa. 40:29).

If a friend is struggling with temptation, strengthen your friend with the words of Paul: "No temptation has overtaken you except what is common to mankind. And God is faithful; he will not let you be tempted beyond what you can bear. But when you are tempted, he will also provide a way out so that you can endure it" (1 Cor. 10:13).

The words God spoke through the psalmist are

especially comforting to those who are going through trials of illness or adversity. "Have mercy on me, LORD, for I am faint; heal me, LORD, for my bones are in agony" (Ps. 6:2). "Praise the LORD, my soul, and forget not all his benefits—who forgives all your sins and heals all your diseases, who redeems your life from the pit and crowns you with love and compassion" (Ps. 103:2–4). And then there's Psalm 23, perhaps the most beautiful and comforting psalm of all, which begins, "The LORD is my shepherd, I lack nothing. He makes me lie down in green pastures, he leads me beside quiet waters, he refreshes my soul."

Most important of all, you may have a friend who needs to hear about the love of God and the atoning death of Jesus on the cross. Always be ready, in season and out of season, to share the words Jesus spoke to the inquiring Nicodemus (John 3:16–17). Jesus said: "For God so loved the world that he gave his one and only Son, that whoever believes in him shall not perish but have eternal life. For God did not send his Son into the world to condemn the world, but to save the world through him."

The Word needs to be communicated *urgently* and applied *relevantly* to the lives of the people around us.

PROCLAIM THE TRUTH
WITH *PATIENCE*

Finally, Paul tells us we must proclaim God's Word "with great *patience* and careful instruction" (2 Tim. 4:2, emphasis added). I must confess, patience is not my strong suit. In fact, this word *patience* is deeply convicting. Many times I have acted impetuously and then repented of my impatience. But even while repenting of my impatience, I've caught myself praying, "Lord, give me patience *right now!*"

What happens when we proclaim God's Word impatiently? All too often, we try to help God's Word. Some try to manipulate people through emotional appeals. People who accept Jesus in the midst of an emotional high are more likely to fall away when emotions subside. In His parable of the sower (Matt. 13), Jesus pictured the gospel as a seed that may fall on rocky places, among thorns, or upon good fertile ground. If we try to manipulate people emotionally who are not ready for the gospel, their faith will not endure.

Some people impatiently resort to a bait-and-switch technique. I heard about a church where neighborhood young people were invited to an evening of fun and games. After an hour or so, the fun stopped and the youth pastor came out to give a gospel presentation. The young people who had come from around the neighborhood weren't told a sermon was part of the evening, and they felt they had been tricked. A game night is a great outreach idea, but if we are impatient and pull a bait and switch on people, they may feel resentful instead of attracted to the gospel.

Proclaiming the Word of God is not a matter of marketing. It's not a matter of techniques. It's not a matter of imitating some program that was successful somewhere else. When we proclaim God's Word, we must speak from our own experience with Christ, our own convictions, and our own authenticity as Christians.

Clever strategies don't convert people to Christ. The Spirit of God converts people, and the Spirit is pleased to use us as partners in the process of converting the world to Christ. But we must be sensitive and open to the Spirit's leading. We need to be receptive channels for the words the Holy Spirit wishes to speak through us.

We don't draw people to Christ. Jesus said, "No one can come to me unless the Father who sent me draws them, and I will raise them up at the last day" (John 6:44). It is God who draws people to Himself, and God alone is responsible for the results, not us. Our faithfulness is not measured by the results we achieve but by our faithfulness in faithfully sharing the good news with others.

Though we are often impatient, God never is. That's why Paul solemnly commands us to proclaim God's Word "with great patience and careful instruction."

THE JUDGMENT OF BELIEVERS

Why did Paul command Timothy to be urgent, relevant, and patient?

First, Paul wants us to be continually aware that God will judge our faithfulness or our lack of faithfulness.

He was facing his own departure from this earth, so the coming judgment was a very real issue for him. Many Christians today do not want to think about God's judgment. They don't want to believe God will examine and judge our lives.

Please understand, the judgment of the believers is not a judgment of punishment in hell. The Scriptures state unequivocally that salvation is by grace through faith alone. We cannot buy, achieve, or earn salvation. Eternal life is a free gift of God's grace. As Paul wrote to the Ephesians:

> For it is by grace you have been saved, through faith—and this is not from yourselves, it is the gift of God—not by works, so that no one can boast. For we are God's handiwork, created in Christ Jesus to do good works, which God prepared in advance for us to do.
>
> —Ephesians 2:8–10

So if we are saved by grace and have nothing to fear from the judgment of sinners, then what is the judgment of the believers? This judgment is our great award ceremony. Each believer will be rewarded differently. God does not believe in socialism. He does not believe in "everyone gets a trophy." He is a fair and just God who rewards His people according to the deeds they have done in life.

All believers are saved by grace, but all believers will not be rewarded equally. As Paul said, we are not *saved* by works, but we are created in Christ Jesus to *do good works.* If people claim to be Christians but do not give themselves to serving God and serving others, if they do not give of their time, talent, and treasure, if they do not live a chaste life and do not walk with God, then even if they are saved, they are in deep trouble. The apostle Paul explained in his first letter to the Corinthians.

> If anyone builds on this foundation using gold, silver, costly stones, wood, hay or straw, their work will be shown for what it is, because the Day will bring it to light. It will be revealed with fire, and the fire will test the quality of each person's work. If what has been built survives, the builder will receive a reward. If it is burned up, the builder will suffer loss but yet will be saved—even though only as one escaping through the flames.
>
> —1 CORINTHIANS 3:12–15

Every believer's work will be tested by fire. God will light a match to all the works we did in this life. If we have lived lives that are lazy, unfaithful, unfruitful, and full of compromise, our works will go up in a puff of smoke. But if we have been faithful believers, using our spiritual gifts, giving of ourselves sacrificially, serving God and others unstintingly, then the fire of God's judgment will make our work shine like molten gold—brighter and purer than any earthly gold. That will be our reward in heaven.

This is why Jesus said in the Sermon on the Mount:

"Do not store up for yourselves treasures on earth, where moths and vermin destroy, and where thieves break in and steal. But store up for yourselves treasures in heaven, where moths and vermin do not destroy, and where thieves do not break in and steal. For where your treasure is, there your heart will be also" (Matt. 6:19–21). Our treasure and our hearts should be in heaven, where God will judge our works and reward us accordingly.

THE UNFAITHFULNESS OF UNBELIEVERS

Second, our proclaiming of the Word must be urgent, relevant, and patient because of the increasing unfaithfulness of people—both inside and outside the church. Paul writes:

> For the time will come when people will not put up with sound doctrine. Instead, to suit their own desires, they will gather around them a great number of teachers to say what their itching ears want to hear. They will turn their ears away from the truth and turn aside to myths.
>
> —2 TIMOTHY 4:3–4

The people Paul describes are among us today. Some of their mottos are: "I'm a Christian, but I don't believe all of the Bible." "I'm a Christian, but I don't accept the Old Testament." "I'm a Christian, but the

God of the Old Testament is not the same as the God of the New Testament." "I am a Christian, but I'm open-minded." "I am a Christian, but I believe all religions lead to God." "I am a Christian, but I like sermons that make me feel good."

Paul says that such people have a pathological condition called "itching ears" (v. 3). They have an itching for novel ideas, for what is trendy, new, makes them feel good, or acceptable to the secular world. They want nothing to do with biblical truth that calls them to repentance.

So they look for a church and a pastor who will tell them what they want to hear. They seek out sermons that affirm them right where they are, that do not require change, repentance, or the atoning blood of Jesus. They want to hear about the love of God, but not His judgment. They want to hear about the grace of God, but not His truth. They only want sermons that will scratch their itching ears.

What is Timothy to do? What are we to do? Paul's answer:

> But you, keep your head in all situations, endure hardship, do the work of an evangelist, discharge all the duties of your ministry
> —2 TIMOTHY 4:5

Remain calm and levelheaded. Endure suffering if you must. Keep preaching and teaching the Word. Do your duty and *never give up on biblical truth.*

In AD 313, when the Roman Emperor Constantine declared the once-persecuted Christian faith to be acceptable, being a Christian suddenly became "fashionable." Immediately, thousands of people who had been secret Christians, who had feared being hunted down, imprisoned, and tortured by the government, came out of the shadows. They were openly baptized and held worship services without fear of official retribution.

At first glance, this might seem to be the best thing to happen to Christianity, but it was not. When Christianity became popular and fashionable, people could call themselves Christians and risk nothing. Before, being a Christian meant being committed to a cause that could get you tortured and killed. Now, however, being a Christian meant belonging to the upper tier of Roman society.

As a result, many people who were not serious about being Christians came into the church. They brought with them the pagan ideas and pagan practices of pre-Christian Rome. Churches became riddled with false ideas that were brought into the church from pagan idolatry.

I'm not saying I prefer living under oppression and persecution. My heart and prayers go out to those today who are facing serious persecution on every continent. And I want you to know that those persecuted Christians in parts of Africa, Asia, the Middle East, and elsewhere are praying for us in the West. They are praying we would remain true and faithful to the gospel.

Some of the Christians I've spoken with in other lands have even told me they are praying for persecution to come to the church in the West. Does that shock you? It shouldn't. They are praying out of love for us that the church in the West would be purified. They told me they pray this way, knowing that when a church grows in favor with the world, it loses its passion for God.

As we look around, as we read and watch the news, we can see these prayers of our brothers and sisters around the world are being answered. Persecution of Christians in Europe and the Americas has begun, including official persecution by the government. As it becomes increasingly unfashionable to be a biblical Christian in the West, we will see a growing apostasy, a growing falling away of people who no longer want to identify as Christians because they never were true Christians in the first place.

I hope and pray the growing persecution in our post-Christian world will neither frighten you nor paralyze you but motivate you to a deeper relationship with the Lord Jesus Christ. I hope and pray as the days grow darker, your faith will grow stronger and your witness for Christ will be increasingly bold.

THE IMPENDING
DEATH OF PAUL

Third, Paul tells Timothy and us that our proclaiming of the Word must be urgent, relevant, and patient because Paul is about to die.

Is Paul sad? No. Is he fearful? No. Paul is eager to be home with the Lord. He is about to die, and Timothy must keep the gospel alive. Paul is in chains, and Timothy must go on preaching the liberating power of Jesus Christ. Paul writes:

> For I am already being poured out like a drink offering, and the time for my departure is near. I have fought the good fight, I have finished the race, I have kept the faith. Now there is in store for me the crown of righteousness, which the Lord, the righteous Judge, will award to me on that day—and not only to me, but also to all who have longed for his appearing.
> —2 TIMOTHY 4:6–8

Paul tells Timothy that the time of his departure is near, and the word he uses for "departure" suggests a ship raising anchor and setting sail for a distant shore. This is how we should look upon the departure of believers. For those who know Jesus Christ as Lord and Savior, death is a promotion from the basement to the penthouse.

The apostle Paul saw his earthly life as a spiritual battlefield. He had been a soldier on that battlefield for a long time. He was battle-scarred and weary. That is why he said, "I have fought the good fight." Like a faithful soldier, Paul had endured the heat of battle.

Some who had been on that battlefield alongside Paul had run away. Some had defected. Some had chosen an easier life without persecution and suffering. Not Paul. He had fought the good fight. He had remained on the front lines.

Paul also compared himself to a marathon runner. "I have finished the race," he wrote. He ran the distance. He refused to quit, no matter how exhausted he felt or how much pain he suffered. He ran his race to the end, not in quest of a wreath for his brow like earthly runners. He ran in quest of a crown his Lord and Savior Jesus Christ would place on his head. Jesus wore a crown of thorns so that He might give a crown of glory to His faithful followers.

And, Paul adds, this crown of righteousness will be given "not only to me, but also to all who have longed for his appearing." Everyone who looks forward to the return of Jesus will receive this crown. Everyone who longs to depart this world and be in the presence of the Lord will receive this crown.

In his 1995 book *Words Aptly Spoken*, Dr. Bob Moorehead, former pastor of Seattle's Overlake Christian Church, told the story of a Christian man in Rwanda in 1980. This was ten years before the Rwandan civil war and genocide, but even then there were fierce tribal and religious tensions in that land. While this Christian man was out walking, he was confronted by a group of armed men who ordered him to renounce Christ or be killed on the spot. He refused to renounce his Lord and Savior, so the armed men struck him down and killed him.

The night before his death, this man had composed a statement of his commitment to following Jesus. The statement was titled "The Fellowship of the Unashamed." Here is what this faithful believer wrote:

> I am part of the "Fellowship of the Unashamed." The die has been cast. I have stepped over the line. The decision has been made. I am a disciple of Jesus Christ. I won't look back, let up, slow down, back away, or be still. My past is redeemed, my present makes sense, and my future is secure. I am finished and done with low living, sight walking, small planning, smooth knees, colorless dreams, chintzy giving, and dwarfed goals.
>
> I no longer need pre-eminence, prosperity, position, promotions, plaudits, or popularity. I now live by presence, lean by faith, love by patience, lift by prayer, and labor by power. My pace is set, my gait is fast, my goal is Heaven, my road is narrow, my way is rough, my companions few, my Guide reliable, my mission clear. I cannot be bought, compromised, deterred, lured away, turned back, diluted, or delayed.
>
> I will not flinch in the face of sacrifice, hesitate in the presence of adversity, negotiate at the

table of the enemy, ponder at the pool of popularity, or meander in the maze of mediocrity.

I am a disciple of Jesus Christ. I must go until Heaven returns, give until I drop, preach until all know, and work until He comes. And when He comes to get His own, He will have no problem recognizing me. My colors will be clear.[3]

These are the words of a man who has settled how he will live and how he will die. These are the words of a man who is eager to do his best and ready to face the worst. This believer faced certain death and refused to deny his Lord.

My prayer is that you and I would be imitators of this Rwandan man, and of the apostle Paul, in the troubled days ahead.

FACING THE END
OF THE WORLD

Unbelievers fear the end of the world. They are afraid the world will end because of global warming, nuclear war, or some future plague far deadlier than COVID-19. They think if they can impose severe environmental restrictions or promote sweeping international agreements, they will somehow be able to save the planet.

They are terrified, and they should be. When the end comes, it will be the most dreadful day. But for those who love Jesus, who long to see Jesus, who eagerly and expectantly look for Jesus, that day will be a day of rejoicing.

Like Paul, let us look forward to our departure. But until that day comes, let's fight the good fight, let's finish our race, and let's *never* give up the faith.

CHAPTER 8

LAST WORDS

WHEN I WAS sixteen years old, our family gathered around my mother's deathbed. It was a profoundly moving moment. My mother kept saying, "I can hear them singing. I can hear them singing."

Then she fell silent, and we all knew she had left this earth and joined the chorus.

Ever since my mother died, I've been fascinated by "last words"—the final thoughts expressed by people just before they depart this life.

I love the story of the final moments of English evangelist John Wesley. After his conversion in 1738, he founded the revival movement known as Methodism, which revolved around small prayer groups, Bible study, and boldly sharing and preaching the gospel. Wesley was also committed to the cause of abolishing slavery. He spent most of his life in poverty because he frequently gave away everything he had. On March 2, 1791, at the age of eighty-seven, he lay on his deathbed with his friends gathered around him. He weakly squeezed the hands of his friends and said, "Farewell,

farewell. The best of all is, God is with us." Then he peacefully slipped away.[1]

And I am moved by the story of the final moments of evangelist Dwight L. Moody. Three days before Christmas 1899, a number of Moody's closest friends and associates gathered around his deathbed. They included hymn writers Ira D. Sankey and George Coles Stebbins, evangelist John R. Mott, and many others. Minutes before his death, Moody opened his eyes and spoke. "Is this dying?" he asked. "Why, this is bliss. There is no valley. I have been within the gates. Earth is receding; Heaven is opening; God is calling; I must go."

Then he fell silent for a while and seemed to be dead. But after a few minutes, he spoke again and said he had been to heaven and seen his loved ones. He mentioned several of them by name. One of his friends suggested he was dreaming. Moody insisted he had been to heaven—it was no dream. Then he died, quietly and at peace.

His friends stayed in the house for a while, talking about Moody's life—and his vision of heaven just before his death. Then, one by one, they each got up and left the house, pondering the last words of Dwight L. Moody.[2]

Some people maintain their sense of humor all the way to their dying moments. It is said that William Sydney Porter—better known as O. Henry, author of many humorous and ironic short stories—was on his deathbed in 1910, surrounded by friends and family, when he seemed to stop breathing.

"Is he dead?" one mourner asked.

"Touch his feet," said another. "Nobody ever died with warm feet."

The dying man startled the mourners by opening his eyes and raising his head from the pillow. "Joan of Arc did," he said. Then he lay back and died.[3]

As we come to the concluding verses of 2 Timothy, we are reading the last recorded words of the great apostle Paul. They may have been written days before he was beheaded in Rome. In his final message to Timothy, Paul underscores the same theme he has woven throughout this letter: *never, never, never* give up on biblical truth.

THE LAST WORDS OF PAUL

As we read the final farewell of the great apostle, it's important to notice not only what he says but what he doesn't say. Nowhere in this closing statement does he ever express a tinge of bitterness, regret, or self-pity. Earlier we read Paul's great statement of triumph and victory:

> For I am already being poured out like a drink offering, and the time for my departure is near. I have fought the good fight, I have finished the race, I have kept the faith. Now there is in store for me the crown of righteousness, which the Lord, the righteous Judge, will award to me on

that day—and not only to me, but also to all who have longed for his appearing.

—2 TIMOTHY 4:6–8

When the time came for Paul to die, he was ready. He did not feel sorry for himself. The only sorrow he felt was over the defection of some of his friends from the faith. He concludes his letter with these words:

Do your best to come to me quickly, for Demas, because he loved this world, has deserted me and has gone to Thessalonica. Crescens has gone to Galatia, and Titus to Dalmatia. Only Luke is with me. Get Mark and bring him with you, because he is helpful to me in my ministry. I sent Tychicus to Ephesus. When you come, bring the cloak that I left with Carpus at Troas, and my scrolls, especially the parchments.

Alexander the metalworker did me a great deal of harm. The Lord will repay him for what he has done. You too should be on your guard against him, because he strongly opposed our message.

At my first defense, no one came to my support, but everyone deserted me. May it not be held against them. But the Lord stood at my side and gave me strength, so that through me the message might be fully proclaimed and all the Gentiles might hear it. And I was delivered from the lion's mouth. The Lord will rescue me from every evil attack and will bring me safely to his heavenly kingdom. To him be glory for ever and ever. Amen.

Greet Priscilla and Aquila and the household of Onesiphorus. Erastus stayed in Corinth, and I left Trophimus sick in Miletus. Do your best to get here before winter. Eubulus greets you, and so do Pudens, Linus, Claudia and all the brothers and sisters.

The Lord be with your spirit. Grace be with you all.

—2 TIMOTHY 4:9–22

Paul lists seventeen different names in this passage. Some deserted him. One, Alexander the metalworker, did him great harm. Most are friends and colleagues in the ministry who are scattered in different cities. Only Dr. Luke, the author of the Gospel of Luke and the Book of Acts, remains with him in Rome. Paul is grateful for Luke's presence, but he longs for contact with many of his other Christian friends. Though Paul never expresses resentment or self-pity, you can hear the anguish and loneliness he feels over being abandoned by some friends and separated from others by great distances.

He expresses the greatest pain over his former companion, a man named Demas. This man is mentioned three times in the New Testament, and those three references paint a picture of a man whose spiritual life is in a downward spiral. He seems to start strong in the Christian faith, but he appears to gradually fall away.

In Philemon verse 24, Paul mentions "Mark, Aristarchus, Demas and Luke, my fellow workers." It takes great commitment to be a fellow worker with Paul, so Demas must have started strong. In Colossians 4:14, Paul mentions him again, saying only that Demas sends greetings to the Colossian church. Then here in 2 Timothy 4:10, a saddened apostle Paul writes, "Demas, because he loved this world, has deserted me and has gone to Thessalonica."

In Paul's day, Thessalonica was a wealthy cosmopolitan city—a center of worldly culture and commerce. Demas was lured away from the work of the gospel by the worldliness of that great city.

Few things are more heartbreaking to a pastor than seeing a once-strong believer fall away from the faith. Nothing breaks the heart of a parent more than a child who wanders away from God. Nothing is more painful to a faithful wife than the spiritual defection of her husband; nothing grieves a faithful husband more deeply than the spiritual defection of his wife.

"Demas, because he loved this world" deserted the Christian faith. May it never be said of you, and may it never be said of me.

IS THERE A "DEMAS" IN YOUR LIFE?

It's not clear if Demas fell into complete unbelief. He might have merely settled for mediocrity. He might have said, "Paul, this missionary life is too hard. I'm just going to move to Thessalonica, start a business, and make some money. I'm not rejecting Jesus. I'm fine with being a mediocre Christian."

I have known a number of Christians who seemed to be on fire for the Lord, but later their zeal for God and their passion for witnessing wore off. And they opted for mediocrity.

We see this again and again in Scripture—believers who for one reason or another settle for mediocrity. Abraham had a disappointing experience with his nephew Lot. It must have broken Abraham's heart to see his nephew make one moral compromise after another, until he narrowly escaped God's judgment against the wicked city of Sodom.

Isaac and Rebekah had a heartbreaking experience with their son Esau. How many sleepless nights must they have spent weeping over Esau's sinful, self-willed choices?

Paul's "Lot," his "Esau," was Demas. In this letter, Paul grieves over Demas because of his decision to chase the mirage of worldly success instead of serving the King of kings. Though Paul is heartbroken over the defection of Demas, there is no indication Paul has given up on Demas. I believe Paul continued to pray that Demas would repent and return to God.

Do you have a "Lot," "Esau," or "Demas" in your life? Have you invested your life in someone, only to receive ingratitude and scorn in return? Is there someone who has broken your heart and wandered from God's will? If so, *don't give up hope*. Don't give up praying for your prodigal. God will answer your prayers and bring your straying loved one to Himself.

Paul writes, "Demas, because he loved this world, has deserted me." He is heartbroken over Demas' defection, so he asks Timothy to come to Rome. As spiritually strong as Paul was, he was not immune to the discouragement that comes from disappointment. Twice in this passage, Paul implores Timothy to make his way to Rome as soon as possible. In verse 9 he says, "Do your best to come to me quickly." His plea is echoed in verse 21, "Do your best to get here before winter."

Because Paul writes so forcefully and commandingly in his letters, it's easy to think of him as invulnerable to the emotions all humans feel. You may know someone in your own life who seems to be rock-solid, invincible, and a tower of strength, yet behind the stoic facade there are times of discouragement and loneliness. We need to be sensitive to those who might seem strong on the outside but are dying on the inside.

When people are going through tough times in a stoic way, consider what they must be going through inside. Go to them with words of encouragement. Pray with them. Weep with them. Let them know they are not alone. Tell them you stand with them and God is with them.

We can all identify with the little boy who was afraid of the dark. His mother told him, "You don't have to be afraid. God is with you."

"I know that," the boy said, "but I want somebody with skin on."

Even though we know God is with us, we all want somebody "with skin on" to be close to us. That's why Paul wanted Timothy to come to Rome soon.

And that's also why I continually encourage Christians to get involved with a small group of believers—a weekly gathering of fellow Christians who study God's Word together, pray for one another, share needs with one another, hold one another accountable, and never share any confidences outside the group. Deep, intense Christian fellowship, which the Greek New Testament calls *koinonia*, is the true biblical model for Christian relationships. When Jesus founded the church, He intended that His followers should live in close fellowship, encouraging one another and carrying one another's burdens, while applying the Word of God to the daily situations of their lives.

You can't experience true *koinonia* fellowship by attending church once or twice a week. Every Christian needs to be in a small-group fellowship. An ideal size for such a group would usually be about eight to fifteen people. These groups often become like a family, frequently sharing meals together and going on retreats to the mountains or the shore. It's important that, in addition to regular Bible study and prayer time, these family-like groups spend time having fun, deepening relationships, and enjoying one another's company.

"WOBBLY" FRIENDS

In this age of social media, people are more connected to one another in superficial ways, yet loneliness is epidemic in our society—and even in the church. Jesus designed His church as a cure for loneliness, a place where believers would always have someone to lean on in times of trouble. The church, as created by God, is the ultimate cure for loneliness.

Years ago I asked a prominent Christian leader, "Do you ever feel lonely?"

He responded, "I'm too busy to be lonely."

A few months later, he called me and said, "I've been reflecting on the question you asked me. I'm afraid my answer was rather glib. The truth is, yes, sometimes I feel *desperately* lonely."

The apostle Paul felt alone and abandoned. Out of his loneliness, he wrote to Timothy, "Do your best to come to me quickly."

It's important to understand that "loneliness" and "alone-ness" are not the same thing. We can be desperately lonely in a room full of people, and we can feel joyful and buoyant in times of complete solitude.

There is the loneliness of leadership, when a leader must make difficult decisions that cannot be delegated to a committee. There is the loneliness of the visionary who discovers no one else shares their vision. There is the loneliness we experience when God calls us to stand against the crowd for biblical truth and godly principles.

Paul understood these forms of loneliness. In verses 16 and 17, he writes, "At my first defense, no one came to my support, but everyone deserted me. May it not be held against them. But the Lord stood at my side and gave me strength." When Paul stood trial in a Roman court of law, he stood alone. No one came to support him.

Even our best friends may go "wobbly" on us when we are under attack from the world. There is no greater sense of loneliness than when our friends abandon us. We all find over time that when the chips are down, there are some friends who stick by us and some who quietly disappear. Some people—even some Christians—are happy to be there for us during good times, when nothing is expected of them. But if life turns up the heat just a little bit, they vanish.

Are you a strong Christian student in high school or college? I have a special word for you. I know your biblical convictions and your witness for Jesus Christ are not popular on campus. I know biblical morality is under assault. If you refuse to compromise your faith and your morality, life on campus can be very lonely.

The Bible tells us, "One who has unreliable friends soon comes to ruin, but there is a friend who sticks closer than a brother" (Prov. 18:24). The friend who sticks closer than a brother is Jesus. He loves you more than you can imagine. He will never abandon you. He is cheering you on. Never surrender your biblical morality. Stick close to Jesus as He sticks close to you.

When you must take a lonely stand for your

convictions, call upon the Lord in prayer and call upon your Christian friends for support. Remember the words of Paul, "But the Lord stood at my side and gave me strength." Paul stands in a long line of men and women who have stood alone for the truth, and as they took their lonely stand, God revealed Himself to them in a supernatural way.

STANDING ALONE FOR GOD

Consider Noah, obediently building a huge ship in the middle of the desert. His neighbors laughed at him and thought he had lost his mind. They called him a religious fanatic, a crazy old man who thought he heard the voice of God. While the rest of the world reveled in drunkenness, sexual immorality, and worse, Noah preached to them, imploring them to repent and turn to God. They responded with mockery and scorn.

Noah made a lonely stand for God in a godless world. And when God opened the windows of heaven, the mockers cried out to Noah, begging for salvation. Noah and his family were safe and dry in the ark of God's protection. But for the rest of the world, it was too late.

The Bible tells us God shut the door of the ark. Not Noah—God (Gen. 7:16). In the same way, those who mock the gospel today will one day find the door of salvation shut forever. Many who believe God would never judge sin, that God will accommodate Himself to their lifestyle, will regret their choices and their rejection of God's truth.

People have actually said to me, "Michael, I can't accept the story of Noah and the ark. What kind of God would shut the door and let people drown?"

I will tell you what kind of God He is. He is a good and loving God who sent His Son to die on the cross for your sins and mine. He is a good and loving God who invites you day after day to turn away from sin and death, and to receive the free gift of eternal life. He is a good and loving God who has blessed you in every way. He is a good and loving God who reaches out to you in love.

If you reject Him and insist on going your own way, what can He do? You have made your own choice.

That is why Paul wrote to the Christians in Rome, "For since the creation of the world God's invisible qualities—his eternal power and divine nature—have been clearly seen, being understood from what has been made, so that people are without excuse" (Rom. 1:20).

That ancient and godly man Job understood the loneliness of abandonment. He suffered the loss of his family, possessions, and health. His friends turned against him and accused him of hidden sin. His wife abandoned him, urging him to curse God and die. Job even came to believe God had abandoned him. But God met Job in the wilderness of his loneliness and spoke to him out of the whirlwind (Job 38:1). God never explained to Job the reason for his sufferings, but God was present in the midst of his sufferings. Ultimately, Job was able to say, "My ears had heard of you but now my eyes have seen you" (Job 42:5).

No matter how bleak your circumstances, no matter how intense your stress and pressure, you are never alone. God is with you. Your church family is with you. Lean on your fellow believers and lean on Jesus.

When I think of loneliness at its worst, I think of Jesus in the Garden of Gethsemane. There, He prayed earnestly and abjectly that the Father would remove from Him the awful cup of the crucifixion. When the guards came to arrest Him, the disciples abandoned Him. He was truly alone. But even greater loneliness lay ahead of him.

He was tried and sentenced to death. He was nailed to the cross—and your sins and mine were placed on Him. At that moment, God the Father turned His face away from Jesus the Son—and Jesus cried out, "My God, my God, why have you forsaken me?" (Matt. 27:46). Those words of Jesus from the cross echo the prophetic words of the psalmist:

> My God, my God, why have you forsaken me?
> Why are you so far from saving me, so far from
> my cries of anguish? My God, I cry out by day,
> but you do not answer, by night, but I find no rest.
> —Psalm 22:1–2

We will never in this life understand the desolate loneliness Jesus felt at that moment. All the light of God's love and favor for Jesus, His beloved Son, was completely extinguished, as if the entire universe had gone dark. Such all-engulfing loneliness is impossible for us to comprehend. The mind recoils from even contemplating it.

The loneliness of Jesus on the cross sanctifies our loneliness. We know we are never truly alone because Jesus fully understands how we feel.

THE CURE FOR LONELINESS

Why doesn't our culture know how to deal with loneliness? Why do so many people around us suffer in silence and loneliness? Why are so many afraid to admit that they are lonely?

Some people—even some Christians—think admitting feelings of loneliness is a sign of weakness. They think others might judge them as "unspiritual" if they were to say, "I feel totally alone right now. I'm going through a trial of loneliness. I need fellowship. I need other people in my life."

In fact, it is a spiritual and godly thing to say to another Christian, "Could we talk? May I share my struggle with you? Would you pray with me? I need believers in my life to let me know I'm not alone. I need encouragement, prayer, and fellowship. I need someone I can trust to hold me accountable, someone I can confess to and confide in."

When Paul was in prison, he needed real fellowship, real Christian friends—not the kind of superficial "friends" you make on Facebook and Instagram, not Twitter followers, but real committed friends who would get down in the trenches with him, who would not forsake him in his time of trial.

Tragically, many of Paul's friends—people he trusted and thought he could count on no matter what—had forsaken him during his trial. Is he bitter? Does he brood over their abandonment and betrayal? No! He prays that they would be forgiven.

Moreover, he writes, "The Lord stood at my side and gave me strength, so that through me the message might be fully proclaimed and all the Gentiles might hear it. And I was delivered from the lion's mouth" (2 Tim. 4:17). This statement reminds us of the warning of the apostle Peter: "Be alert and of sober mind. Your enemy the devil prowls around like a roaring lion looking for someone to devour" (1 Pet. 5:8).

Satan had set traps for the apostle Paul. At his trial and during his imprisonment, Paul was on the spiritual battlefield, facing his spiritual enemy and fighting the good fight. Satan tried to use Paul's trial of abandonment as a weapon to weaken Paul's faith. Satan tried to get Paul to turn his back on biblical truth. If Paul was discouraged, fearful, and lonely enough, he might say whatever his Roman accusers wanted him to say, just to save his own skin.

But Paul rejoiced that Satan's scheme failed. The Lord was at his side, giving him strength, and Paul boldly proclaimed the gospel in that courtroom so that all the Gentiles present might hear God's truth. And he was delivered from the lion's mouth—the trap of Satan.

Paul was not delivered from the Roman prison. He was not delivered from the threat of execution. He was not delivered from the cold, filth, squalor, and stench of his cell. But he was delivered from the scheme of Satan. The Word of God went forth, even in Paul's weakness and imprisonment.

In your times of loneliness, beware. Satan may be setting his traps for you. This is no time to abandon Christian fellowship. This is no time to abandon prayer and the study of God's Word. Satan wants you to think you're all alone, your faith is meaningless, and your commitment to God's truth is foolish and impractical.

When you're going through your own private Gethsemane—your own trial of loneliness because of your obedience to God's Word—gather your Christian friends close. You need the fellowship, prayers, and encouragement of other Christians now more than ever. Their presence in your life will affirm God's promises to you.

Then you'll be able to say with the apostle Paul, "The Lord will rescue me from every evil attack and will bring me safely to his heavenly kingdom. To him be glory for ever and ever. Amen" (2 Tim. 4:18).

When you study the life and letters of the apostle Paul, one truth becomes glaringly obvious. Paul's greatest fear was that he might do something that would cost him his reward in heaven. He worried he might somehow disgrace the name of the Lord. His greatest longing was to run his race to the finish line.

He wanted nothing more than to finish well and give glory to the Lord.

That is the great passion of my heart. I hope it is your longing too.

BETTER TO BE ALONE
WITH GOD

Do you know the story of Joan of Arc? During the closing decades of the Hundred Years' War between France and England, Joan, a peasant girl in France, began having visions of the archangel Michael, Saint Margaret, and Saint Catherine of Alexandria. She had her first vision in 1425, when she was thirteen years old. She said that, in the visions, she received instructions for liberating France from English domination.

In 1428, when she was sixteen, she petitioned the French royal court at Chinon, asking for an audience with King Charles VII. She wanted to tell the king about her visions. After more than a year of persistent asking, she was finally allowed to meet the king in 1429. She impressed the king and persuaded him that her visions held the key to victory. A panel of clergy investigated young Joan and found her to be a good Christian girl who possessed "virtues of humility, honesty, and simplicity."

King Charles VII placed Joan in charge of an army that marched to Orléans, where English forces had besieged the city for seven months. England was at the height of its powers and there seemed no hope of a French victory. But with Joan of Arc leading the French army, the English siege was broken in just nine days. This was the first of several military victories won by French forces led by a teenage girl who saw visions.

In May 1430, Joan was captured by French traitors and handed over to the English. She was put on trial by a pro-English bishop, Pierre Cauchon. She was just nineteen years old. At her trial, her friends and family members abandoned her. They knew she would probably be executed, and they were afraid to speak up and share her fate.

In George Bernard Shaw's play *Saint Joan*, he pictures the scene where Joan faces trial and execution. She asks the army comrades who fought alongside her to stand up and defend her. But they will not. They abandon her to her fate. So she tells them:

> I am alone on earth: I have always been alone....
> In my innocence I believed that you who now
> cast me out would be like strong towers to keep
> harm from me. But I am wiser now; and nobody
> is any the worse for being wiser....My loneliness
> shall be my strength....It is better to be alone
> with God; His friendship will not fail me, nor
> His counsel, nor His love....And so, God be
> with me![4]

Abandoned by friends and family, she stood trial alone and was condemned to be burned at the stake. Though her speech was written by a playwright, I believe that speech captured the courageous, faithful heart of young Joan as she faced torture and death: "It is better to be alone with God."

Friend in Christ, in the days to come, you and I may be called to stand alone for God's truth. Our friends and family may forsake us, but God's friendship will never fail. The love of people may grow cold, but the love of God sustains us, just as God's love sustained the apostle Paul.

It's easy and natural to go with the flow, but it's supernatural and godly to stand alone. It's easy and natural to drift with the tide, but it's supernatural and godly to stand against the tide. It's easy and natural to compromise and make friends with the world, but it's supernatural and godly to *reject* compromise and *refuse* to surrender. It is better to be alone with God.

These were Paul's last words to Timothy. His final letter was a message of encouragement—and command: *Never, ever give up!*

Never give up on prayer.

Never give up on biblical truth.

Never give up on the infallibility of the Word of God.

Never give up on the faith that was once delivered.

Never give up on sound doctrine.

Press on, persevere, and don't ever give up.

Even when everyone else forsakes you, God is with you. And it is better to be alone with God. He will deliver you from the lion's mouth. He will rescue you from every evil attack. He will safely bring you to His heavenly kingdom and your eternal home.

NOTES

Chapter 1
Encouraging Words for Discouraging Times

1. Anonymous, "George Muller Persistent Prayer for 5 Individuals," GeorgeMuller.org, July 3, 2017, https://www.georgemuller.org/devotional/george-muller-persistent-prayer-for-5-individuals.

2. "David Platt Is Harming McLean Bible Church With Woke Social Justice Theology," Capstone Report, June 9, 2021, https://capstonereport.com/2021/06/09/david-platt-is-harming-mclean-bible-church-with-woke-social-justice-theology/36219/.

3. Meeke Addison, "The Stated Goals of Black Lives Matter Are Anti-Christian," *Decision Magazine*, July 1, 2020, https://decisionmagazine.com/the-stated-goals-of-black-lives-matter-are-anti-christian/.

4. Joseph Farah, "Pastor Insults President Trump? It Gets Much Worse at McLean Bible Church," WND, August 9, 2021, https://www.wnd.com/2021/08/pastor-insults-president-trump-gets-much-worse-mclean-bible-church/.

5. "David Platt Is Harming McLean Bible Church With Woke Social Justice Theology," Capstone Report; James White, "Nearly Two Hours on Critical Race Theory, White Privilege, T4G, and

More," podcast, April 17, 2018, https://www.
aomin.org/aoblog/christian-worldview/nearly-two-
hours-on-critical-race-theory-white-privilege-t4g-
and-more/.

6. C. S. Lewis, *Mere Christianity* (New York:
    HarperOne, 2001), 134.

7. Madeleine Davies, "Celebration at News of
    Archbishop of York Appointment," *Church Times*,
    December 20, 2019, https://www.churchtimes.
    co.uk/articles/2019/20-december/news/uk/
    celebration-at-news-of-archbishop-of-york-
    appointment.

8. "New Archbishop of York: 'Bible Has to Fit
    the Current Culture,'" The Christian Institute,
    December 18, 2019, https://www.christian.org.uk/
    news/new-archbishop-of-york-bible-has-to-fit-the-
    current-culture/.

9. Melvin Tinker, "Stephen Cottrell: A Crisis of
    Confidence," *Christian Concern*, December 19,
    2019, https://christianconcern.com/comment/
    stephen-cottrell-a-crisis-of-confidence/.

10. *Merriam-Webster*, s.v. "sanctify," accessed November
    4, 2021, https://www.merriam-webster.com/
    dictionary/sanctify.

Chapter 2
Do Not Be Ashamed

1. Minyvonne Burke, "Virginia Teacher Reinstated
    After Speaking Out Against School Pronoun

Policy," NBC Universal, June 9, 2021, https://
www.nbcnews.com/news/us-news/virginia-
teacher-reinstated-after-speaking-out-against-
school-pronoun-policy-n1270127; Jonathan
Turley, "'A Matter of Public Concern:' Virginia
Judge Orders Reinstatement of Teacher Who
Criticized Gender Policy," JonathanTurley.
org, June 8, 2021, https://jonathanturley.
org/2021/06/08/a-matter-of-public-concern-
virginia-judge-orders-reinstatement-of-teacher-
who-criticized-gender-policy/.

2. "Gender Neutral Pronouns," LGBTQ+ Student
Center, University of Southern California,
accessed November 4, 2021, https://lgbtrc.usc.edu/
education/trans-identities/transgender/pronouns/.

3. Keri D. Ingraham, "The Radical Reshaping of
K-12 Public Education: Gender Redefinition and
Self-Selection," *American Spectator*, June 1, 2021,
https://spectator.org/public-schools-gender-radical-
reshaping/.

4. Robert Karen, "Shame," *The Atlantic Monthly* 269,
no. 2 (February 1992): 40.

5. Josh Harris (harrisjosh), Instagram, July 26, 2019,
https://www.instagram.com/p/B0ZBrNLH2sl/.

Chapter 3
Soldiers, Farmers, and Athletes for Truth

1. Bonnie Kristian, "The Coming End of Christian
America," *The Week*, October 21, 2019, https://

theweek.com/articles/872709/coming-end-christian-america.

2. "Poster—All 266 Popes From Peter to Francis—Roman Catholic Church—24x36," The Mad Papist, accessed November 5, 2021, https://www.amazon.com/Pope-Poster-Popes-Peter-Francis/dp/B0142YAO6Y/.

Chapter 4
We Have an Enemy

1. Jennifer Senior, "In Conversation: Antonin Scalia," *New York*, October 4, 2013, https://nymag.com/news/features/antonin-scalia-2013-10/index3.html.

2. C. S. Lewis, *The Screwtape Letters* (New York: Macmillan, 1943), 13.

Chapter 5
The Last Days

1. William Dannemeyer, *Shadow in the Land: Homosexuality in America* (San Francisco: Ignatius Press, 1989), 85–86.

2. Jonathan Turley, "Hannah-Jones: 'All Journalism Is Activism,'" JonathanTurley.org, July 20, 2021, https://jonathanturley.org/2021/07/20/hannah-jones-all-journalism-is-activism/.

3. "Pastors Face Communication Challenges in a Divided Culture," Barna Group Inc., January 29, 2019, https://www.barna.com/research/pastors-speaking-out/.

4. Leading The Way, "Michael Youssef on *Fox & Friends* (April 10, 2019)–'If It's in the Bible, I'm Going to Preach It,'" YouTube, April 10, 2019, https://www.youtube.com/watch?v=BXPPF5sLvy8.

Chapter 6
The Pressure to Conform

1. Fred the Oyster, "File:Asch experiment.svg," Wikimedia Commons, accessed November 11, 2021, https://commons.wikimedia.org/wiki/File:Asch_experiment.svg. Used with permission.

2. Saul McLeod, "Solomon Asch—Conformity Experiment," *Simply Psychology*, December 28, 2018, https://www.simplypsychology.org/asch-conformity.html.

3. GracePointe Church (@gracepointetn), "As Progressive Christians, we're open to...," Facebook, February 7, 2021, https://m.facebook.com/gracepointetn/photos/a.394837242014/101574 95440607015/?type=3.

4. GracePointe Church (@gracepointetn), "As Progressive Christians, we're open to...."

5. Alban Butler, *The Lives of the Fathers, Martyrs, and Other Principal Saints* (Dublin: James Duffy, 1866), https://www.bartleby.com/210/10/242.html. Note: This source refers to Felix's home city as Thiabara, but most historical sources refer to it as Thibiuca.

Chapter 7
Facing the Coming Judgment

1. R. Albert Mohler Jr., "We Have Seen All This Before: Rob Bell and the (Re)Emergence of Liberal Theology," *Christian Post*, March 18, 2011, https://www.christianpost.com/news/we-have-seen-all-this-before-rob-bell-and-the-reemergence-of-liberal-theology.html.

2. Mohler Jr., "We Have Seen All This Before: Rob Bell and the (Re)Emergence of Liberal Theology."

3. "The Fellowship of the Unashamed," The Gospel Truth, accessed November 9, 2021, https://www.gospeltruth.net/unashamed.htm, quoted in Bob Moorehead, *Words Aptly Spoken* (Kirkland, WA: Overlake Press, 1995).

Chapter 8
Last Words

1. John Fletcher Hurst, *John Wesley the Methodist: A Plain Account of His Life and Work* (New York: Methodist Book Concern, 1903), 298.

2. J. Wilbur Chapman, *The Life & Work of Dwight Lyman Moody* (London: James Nisbet & Co., Limited, 1900), 416.

3. Sandra Martin, et al., "What Are the Best Last Words Ever?," *The Atlantic*, April 2016, https://www.theatlantic.com/magazine/archive/2016/04/what-are-the-best-last-words-ever/471522/.

4. David Hlavsa, *An Actor Rehearses: What to Do When—and Why* (New York: Allworth Press, 2006), 42.

A FREE GIFT for You

Thank you for reading my book. I pray it has brought you hope and encouragement to never give up on the truth of God's Word.

As a thank-you, I am offering you the e-book *Hope for This Present Crisis* **FOR FREE!**

Discover the seven-step prescription to restoring sanity in a world gone mad.

To get this **FREE** gift, please go to **www.dryoussefbooks.com/gift**.

Scan with smartphone

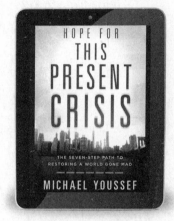

Many thanks, and God bless,

Michael Youssef